# First World War
and Army of Occupation
War Diary
France, Belgium and Germany

3 DIVISION
Headquarters, Branches and Services
Royal Army Veterinary Corps
Deputy Assistant Director Veterinary Services
13 May 1915 - 30 June 1919

WO95/1398/2

The Naval & Military Press Ltd
www.nmarchive.com
Published in association with The National Archives

Published by

The Naval & Military Press Ltd

Unit 10 Ridgewood Industrial Park,

Uckfield, East Sussex,

TN22 5QE England

Tel: +44 (0) 1825 749494

www.naval-military-press.com

www.nmarchive.com

This diary has been reprinted in facsimile from the original. Any imperfections are inevitably reproduced and the quality may fall short of modern type and cartographic standards.

© **Crown Copyright**
Images reproduced by permission of The National Archives, London, England, 2015.

Contents

Document type	Place/Title	Date From	Date To
Heading	WO95/1398-1		
Heading	3rd Division Divl. Troops Dep. Asst Dir. Ord. Services 1915 May-1919 June		
Heading	3rd Div D. O.O War Diary May-Dec 1915		
Heading	D.O.O. 3rd Division Vol I 13-31.5.15		
War Diary	Westoutre	13/05/1915	30/05/1915
War Diary	Busse Boom	31/05/1915	31/05/1915
Heading	3rd Division DADOS. 3rd Division Vol II 1-30.6.15		
War Diary	Busse Boom	01/06/1915	03/06/1915
War Diary	Poperinghe	04/06/1915	30/06/1915
Heading	3rd Division D.A.D.O.S. 3rd Division Vol III		
Heading	War Diary of D.A.D.O.S. 3rd Division (Major H.S. Bush A.O.D) From 1.7.15 To 31.7.15		
War Diary	Poperinghe	01/07/1915	29/07/1915
War Diary	Reninghelst	30/07/1915	31/07/1915
Heading	War Diary of D.A.D.O.S. III Division From 1st To 31st Aug 1915 Vol IV 3rd Division		
War Diary	Reninghelst	01/08/1915	31/08/1915
Heading	3rd Division War Diary of D.A.D.O.S. 3rd Div (Lt. Col. H.S. Bush A.O.D) from 1/9/15 to 30/9/15 Vol V		
War Diary	Reninghelst	30/08/1915	30/09/1915
Heading	3rd Division War Diary of D.A.D.O.S. 3rd Division From 1-10-15 To 31-10-15 Vol VI		
War Diary	Reninghelst	01/10/1915	22/10/1915
War Diary	Steenvoorde	23/10/1915	31/10/1915
Heading	3rd Division War Diary of D.A.D.O.S. 3rd Div from 29-10-15 To 30-11-15 Vol VII		
War Diary	Steenvoorde	29/10/1915	21/11/1915
War Diary	Reninghelst	22/11/1915	30/11/1915
Heading	D.A.D.O.S. 3rd Divn. Dec Vol VIII		
War Diary	Reninghelst	01/12/1915	31/12/1915
Heading	3rd Division Divl. Troops D.A.D.O.S. Jan-Dec 1916		
Heading	D A D O S 3rd Div Jan Vol IX		
War Diary	Reninghelst	01/01/1916	31/01/1916
Heading	War Diary of D.A.D.O.S. 3rd Division From 1-2-16 To 29-2-16 Vol 19		
War Diary	Reninghelst	01/02/1916	06/02/1916
War Diary	Nordausques	07/02/1916	29/02/1916
Heading	War Diary of D.A.D.O.S. 3rd Division From 1-3-16 To 31-3-16 Vol XX		
War Diary	Nordausques	01/03/1916	08/03/1916
War Diary	Reninghelst	09/03/1916	31/03/1916
Heading	War Diary of D.A.D.O.S. 3rd Division From 1-4-16 To 30-4-16 Vol 12		
War Diary	Reninghelst	01/04/1916	02/04/1916
War Diary	Fletre	03/04/1916	26/04/1916
War Diary	Westoutre	27/04/1916	30/04/1916
Heading	War Diary of D.A.D.O.S. 3rd Division From 1-5-16 To 31-5-16 Vol 22		
War Diary	Westoutre	01/05/1916	27/05/1916

War Diary	Fletre	28/05/1916	31/05/1916
Heading	War Diary of D.A.D.O.S. 3rd Division From 1-6-16 To 30-6-16 Vol 23		
War Diary	Fletre	01/06/1916	18/06/1916
War Diary	Tilques	19/06/1916	30/06/1916
Heading	War Diary of D.A.D.O.S. 3rd Division From 1-7-16 To 31-7-16 Vol 24		
War Diary	Tilques	01/07/1916	02/07/1916
War Diary	Le Meillard	03/07/1916	03/07/1916
War Diary	Flesselles	04/07/1916	04/07/1916
War Diary	Corbie	05/07/1916	08/07/1916
War Diary	Bray Sur Somme	09/07/1916	27/07/1916
War Diary	Treux	28/07/1916	31/07/1916
Heading	War Diary of D.A.D.O.S. 3rd Division From 1-8-16 To 31-8-16 Vol 25		
War Diary	Treux (Somme)	01/08/1916	12/08/1916
War Diary	Grovetown (Somme)	13/08/1916	13/08/1916
War Diary	Forked Tree (Somme)	14/08/1916	22/08/1916
War Diary	Treux (Somme)	23/08/1916	23/08/1916
War Diary	Bernaville (Somme)	24/08/1916	25/08/1916
War Diary	Frohen Le Grand (Somme)	26/08/1916	26/08/1916
War Diary	Flers	27/08/1916	27/08/1916
War Diary	Noeux Les Mines	28/08/1916	31/08/1916
Heading	War Diary of D.A.D.O.S. 3rd Div 1-9-16 To 30-9-16 Vol 26		
War Diary	Noeux Les Mines	01/09/1916	22/09/1916
War Diary	Bomy	23/09/1916	30/09/1916
Heading	War Diary of D.A.D.O.S. 3rd Division From 1-10-16 To 31-10-16 Vol 27		
War Diary	Bomy	01/10/1916	05/10/1916
War Diary	On Move South	06/10/1916	06/10/1916
War Diary	Bertrancourt (Somme)	07/10/1916	10/10/1916
War Diary	Bertrancourt	11/10/1916	17/10/1916
War Diary	Bus Les Artois	19/10/1916	30/11/1916
Heading	War Diary of D.A.D.O.S. 3rd Division From 1-12-16 To 31-12-16 Vol 29		
War Diary	Bus Les Artois	01/12/1916	31/12/1916
Heading	3rd Division Divl. Troops Dep. Asst Dir. Ordnance Services Jan-Dec 1917		
Heading	War Diary of D.A.D.O.S. 3rd Division From 1-1-17 To 31-1-17 Vol 30		
War Diary	Bus Les Artois	01/01/1917	08/01/1917
War Diary	Canaples	08/01/1917	29/01/1917
War Diary	Third Army	29/01/1917	30/01/1917
War Diary	Third Army On Move	30/01/1917	30/01/1917
War Diary	Villers Chatel	31/01/1917	31/01/1917
Heading	War Diary of D.A.D.O.S. 3rd Division From 1-2-17 To 28-2-17 Vol 31		
War Diary	Villers Chatel	02/02/1917	08/02/1917
War Diary	Lignereuil	08/02/1917	11/02/1917
War Diary	Warlus	11/02/1917	28/02/1917
Heading	War Diary of D.A.D.O.S. 3rd Division From 1/3/17 To 31/3/17 Vol 32		
War Diary	Warlus	01/03/1917	31/03/1917
Heading	War Diary D.A.D.O.S. 3rd Div Period 1-4-17 To 30-4-17 Vol 33		

War Diary	Warlus	01/04/1917	10/04/1917
War Diary	Warlus Arras	11/04/1917	17/04/1917
War Diary	Warlus	18/04/1917	22/04/1917
War Diary	Warlus Arras	23/04/1917	25/04/1917
War Diary	Arras	26/04/1917	30/04/1917
Heading	War Diary D.A.D.O.S. 3rd Division From 1-5-17 To 31-5-17 Vol 34		
War Diary	Arras	01/05/1917	15/05/1917
War Diary	Warlus	15/05/1917	19/05/1917
War Diary	Lignereuil	19/05/1917	19/05/1917
War Diary	Lignereuil	20/05/1917	31/05/1917
Heading	War Diary D.A.D.O.S. 3rd Division Capt D.J. Jack ADD From 1.6.17 To 30.6.17 Vol 35		
Miscellaneous	D.A.G 3rd Echelon Base	01/07/1917	01/07/1917
War Diary	Lignereuil	01/06/1917	02/06/1917
War Diary	Arras	02/06/1917	20/06/1917
War Diary	Le-Cauroy	20/06/1917	30/06/1917
Heading	Captain D.J.Jack D.O.D. D.O.D.D.S. 3rd Div War Diary form 1.7.17 To 31.7.17 Vol 36		
Miscellaneous	D.A.G. 3rd Echelon Base	01/08/1917	01/08/1917
War Diary	Le-Cauroy	01/07/1917	01/07/1917
War Diary	Fremicourt	01/07/1917	31/07/1917
Miscellaneous	The D.A.G. Base	31/08/1917	31/08/1917
War Diary	Fremicourt	01/08/1917	31/08/1917
Miscellaneous	D.A.G. 3rd Echelon	01/10/1917	01/10/1917
War Diary	Fremicourt	01/09/1917	06/09/1917
War Diary	Rocquigny	07/09/1917	17/09/1917
War Diary	Watou	17/09/1917	24/09/1917
War Diary	Poperinghe	24/09/1917	29/09/1917
War Diary	Poperinghe Winnezeele	30/09/1917	30/09/1917
Miscellaneous	D.A.G. 3rd Echelon	31/10/1917	31/10/1917
War Diary	Winnizeele	01/10/1917	04/10/1917
War Diary	Renescure	04/10/1917	06/10/1917
War Diary	Barastre	06/10/1917	12/10/1917
War Diary	Monument Commomoratif	13/10/1917	31/10/1917
Heading	D.A.G. 3rd Echelon for Month of November 1917		
War Diary	Monument Commomoratif	01/11/1917	30/11/1917
Miscellaneous	D.A.G 3rd Echelon	31/12/1917	31/12/1917
War Diary	Monument Commomoratif	01/12/1917	14/12/1917
War Diary	Monument Commomoratif Ervillers	15/12/1917	15/12/1917
War Diary	Ervillers	16/12/1917	28/01/1918
War Diary	Boisleux-au-Mont	29/01/1918	31/01/1918
Miscellaneous	D.A.G 3rd Echelon	28/02/1918	28/02/1918
War Diary	Boisleux-au-Mont	01/02/1918	28/02/1918
Miscellaneous	D A G 3rd Echelon	31/03/1918	31/03/1918
War Diary	Boisleux-au-Mont	01/03/1918	21/03/1918
War Diary	Riviere	22/03/1918	27/03/1918
War Diary	Barly	28/03/1918	31/03/1918
Miscellaneous	D A G 3rd Echelon	30/04/1918	30/04/1918
War Diary	Barly	01/04/1918	01/04/1918
War Diary	Bruay	02/04/1918	03/04/1918
War Diary	Labeuvriere	04/04/1918	05/04/1918
War Diary	Fouquieres	06/04/1918	08/04/1918
War Diary	Labeuvriere	09/04/1918	11/04/1918
War Diary	Busnettes	12/04/1918	12/04/1918
War Diary	Burbure	13/04/1918	16/04/1918

War Diary	Labeuvriere	17/04/1918	30/04/1918
Miscellaneous	D.A.G 3rd Echelon	31/05/1918	31/05/1918
War Diary	Labeuvriere	01/05/1918	31/05/1918
Miscellaneous	D.A.G 3rd Echelon	30/06/1918	30/06/1918
War Diary	Labeuvriere	01/06/1918	01/06/1918
War Diary	Lapugnoy	02/06/1918	30/06/1918
Miscellaneous	D.A.G 3rd Echelon	31/07/1918	31/07/1918
War Diary	Lapugnoy	01/07/1918	31/07/1918
Miscellaneous	D.A.G G.H.Q 3rd Echelon	31/08/1918	31/08/1918
War Diary	Bois De Mareque	01/08/1918	06/08/1918
War Diary	Bellery	06/08/1918	13/08/1918
War Diary	Bavincourt	13/08/1918	20/08/1918
War Diary	Saulty	20/08/1918	27/08/1918
War Diary	La Cauchie	27/08/1918	29/08/1918
War Diary	Boiry St Martin	29/08/1918	06/09/1918
War Diary	Humbercamp	06/09/1918	07/09/1918
Miscellaneous	D.A.G 3rd Echelon	30/09/1918	30/09/1918
War Diary	Humbercamp	08/09/1918	12/09/1918
War Diary	Gomiecourt	12/09/1918	15/09/1918
War Diary	Beugny	15/09/1918	01/10/1918
War Diary	Flesquieres	01/10/1918	08/10/1918
War Diary	Hermies	09/10/1918	13/10/1918
War Diary	Marcoing	13/10/1918	20/10/1918
War Diary	Cattenieres	20/10/1918	21/10/1918
War Diary	Quievy	21/10/1918	24/10/1918
War Diary	Solesmes	24/10/1918	31/10/1918
War Diary	Quievy	31/10/1918	31/10/1918
Miscellaneous	D.A.G 3rd Echelon	30/11/1918	30/11/1918
War Diary	Quievy	01/11/1918	09/11/1918
War Diary	Frasnoy	10/11/1918	18/11/1918
War Diary	Sous-Le-Bois	19/11/1918	23/11/1918
War Diary	Cousolre	24/11/1918	24/11/1918
War Diary	Thuin	25/11/1918	25/11/1918
War Diary	Louveral	26/11/1918	27/11/1918
War Diary	Bioul	28/11/1918	29/11/1918
War Diary	Emptinne	30/11/1918	30/11/1918
Miscellaneous	D.A.G 3rd Echelon	01/01/1919	01/01/1919
War Diary	Emptinne	01/12/1918	05/12/1918
War Diary	Grand Han	06/12/1918	06/12/1918
War Diary	Salmchateau	07/12/1918	13/12/1918
War Diary	Losheim	14/12/1918	16/12/1918
War Diary	Euskirchen	17/12/1918	20/12/1918
War Diary	Duren	21/12/1918	31/12/1918
Heading	Northern Division (Late 3rd Division) D.A. Dir. Ord. Services 1919 Jan-Jun 1919		
Miscellaneous	D.A.G 3rd Echelon	01/02/1919	01/02/1919
War Diary	Duren	01/01/1919	28/02/1919
War Diary	Cologne	01/06/1919	30/06/1919

WO 57/1398(1)

**3RD DIVISION
DIVL. TROOPS**

DEP. ASST DIR. ORD. SERVICES.
~~May 1915~~
~~Dec 1918~~

1915 MAY — 1919 JUNE

SUBJECT.

No.	Contents.	Date.
	3rd DIV. D.O.O. WAR DIARY, MAY - DEC, 1915	

D.A.A. 3rd Division

Vol I. 13 — 31.5.15

WAR DIARY
or
INTELLIGENCE SUMMARY.
(Erase heading not required.)

Army Form C. 2118.

Instructions regarding War Diaries and Intelligence Summaries are contained in F.S. Regs., Part II. and the Staff Manual respectively. Title pages will be prepared in manuscript.

Hour, Date, Place	Summary of Events and Information	Remarks and references to Appendices
13.5.15. WESTOUTRE	Two 4.7 Guns arrived vice hand for 116 Heavy Battery. Drawn and taken away by battery on arrival. Also one truck load of stores. Mr Bowen took over issuing Foreman from Mr Sims, who left for England. S/SS Hamley took over duty of collecting stores from Railhead. 25% of blankets ordered to be returned by troops, now coming in — weather wet.	
14.5.15. "	One truck load of stores arrived. Also 3 G.S. wagons for Tr.O.Pr. Coy. 3rd Divl. Train and 1 Batn Cart for 2/Leicestershire 42nd Bde from "G" Coy. Taken over and delivered to units forthwith. L/Cpl Holland arrived from 27th Div n and reported for duty and was posted to 9th Brigade.	

Army Form C. 2118.

WAR DIARY
or
INTELLIGENCE SUMMARY.
(Erase heading not required.)

Instructions regarding War Diaries and Intelligence Summaries are contained in F.S. Regs., Part II. and the Staff Manual respectively. Title pages will be prepared in manuscript.

Hour, Date, Place	Summary of Events and Information	Remarks and references to Appendices
15/5/15 Westoutre	Vickers Gun in charge of #"P"Hopkins rendered "W". Demand submitted to Base and 19495. 1 Truck load of Stores received.	/MS
16/5/15 Westoutre	New Vickers Gun arrived for 2nd Royal Scots to replace W. Gun. 10.O.O.S. informed 1 Truck load of Stores arrived 100 Birman Slitters transpt to 5th 10in	/MS
17/5/15 Westoutre	1 Truck load of Stores arrived Demands for Cable & Electric to be dealt with in accordance with procedure for Telephones (G20/659) G20/851.	/MS

Army Form C. 2118.

WAR DIARY
or
INTELLIGENCE SUMMARY.
(Erase heading not required.)

Instructions regarding War Diaries and Intelligence Summaries are contained in F.S. Regs., Part II. and the Staff Manual respectively. Title pages will be prepared in manuscript.

Hour, Date, Place	Summary of Events and Information	Remarks and references to Appendices
18-5-15 Westoutre	1 Truck load of Stores arrived, also Water Cart for 115th Battery and portion of Coker for 1st Indium. 1 Water Cart demanded from Base for 2/R.I.Rifles	JMS
19-5-15 Westoutre	1 Truck load of Stores arrived. Qd. Commn. notify supplies of Respirators arriving and exist in failure to demand in Bulk in demands.	
20-5-15 Westoutre	1 Truck load of Stores arrived - including new Vickers Guns for 4th R.I.Fusiliers. Demand submitted to Base for Machine Gun ½ S.Lancs. 10,000 S. notifies that Respirators now obtainable in demand from Base. 10,000 demanded "Bulk" D.O.O. went to Army Hd Qrs to interview D.D.O.S.	JMS

Forms/C. 2118/10

Army Form C. 2118.

WAR DIARY
or
INTELLIGENCE SUMMARY.
(Erase heading not required.)

Instructions regarding War Diaries and Intelligence Summaries are contained in F.S. Regs., Part II. and the Staff Manual respectively. Title pages will be prepared in manuscript.

Hour, Date, Place	Summary of Events and Information	Remarks and references to Appendices
21-5-15 Westoutre	One truck load of Stores arrived. Machine Gun of the Div. damaged by rifle fire - repairs carried out in Armourers Shop	
22-5-15 Westoutre	One truck load of Stores arrived. Sent lorry to St. Omer to draw 1000 Respirators.	
23-5-15 Westoutre	One Truck load of Stores arrived	
24-5-15 Westoutre	One Truck load of Stores arrived 2500 Respirators (Reserve) demanded from Base	

Army Form C. 2118.

WAR DIARY
or
INTELLIGENCE SUMMARY.
(Erase heading not required.)

Instructions regarding War Diaries and Intelligence Summaries are contained in F.S. Regs., Part II. and the Staff Manual respectively. Title pages will be prepared in manuscript.

Hour, Date, Place	Summary of Events and Information	Remarks and references to Appendices
25-5-15 WESTOUTRE	No Stores from Base. 3000 Respirators demanded from Base - to complete first issues.	
26-5-15 WESTOUTRE	Received 10500 Respirators from St Omer (7500 for Div Reserve) One truck load of stores arrived. Div:n Now complete with respirators.	

Army Form C. 2118.

WAR DIARY
or
INTELLIGENCE SUMMARY.
(Erase heading not required.)

Instructions regarding War Diaries and Intelligence Summaries are contained in F.S. Regs., Part II. and the Staff Manual respectively. Title pages will be prepared in manuscript.

Hour, Date, Place	Summary of Events and Information	Remarks and references to Appendices
27.5.15 WESTOUTRE	One truck load of Stores arrived. 13 G.S. Wagons - complete Transports arrived for Armoured Train, to replace one Horse Hay Carts. Sub Conr. Brennan left for Havre en route to England.	
28.5.15 WESTOUTRE	One truck load of stores arrived	
29.5.15 WESTOUTRE	One truck load of Stores arrived also Machine Gun for 2/S. Lancs	

Forms/C. 2118/10

Army Form C. 2118.

WAR DIARY
or
INTELLIGENCE SUMMARY.

(Erase heading not required.)

Instructions regarding War Diaries and Intelligence Summaries are contained in F.S. Regs., Part II. and the Staff Manual respectively. Title pages will be prepared in manuscript.

Hour, Date, Place	Summary of Events and Information	Remarks and references to Appendices
30-5-15 WESTOUTRE	One truck load of Stores arrived	JMS
31-5-15 BUSSE BOOM	Moved from WESTOUTRE to BUSSE BOOM. One truck load of Stores arrived	JMS

3rd Division

DADOS. 3rd Division

Vol II 1 — 30.6.15.

Army Form C. 2118.

WAR DIARY
or
INTELLIGENCE SUMMARY.
(Erase heading not required.)

Instructions regarding War Diaries and Intelligence Summaries are contained in F.S. Regs., Part II. and the Staff Manual respectively. Title pages will be prepared in manuscript.

Hour, Date, Place	Summary of Events and Information	Remarks and references to Appendices
1-6-15 BUSSE BOOM	One truck load of stores arrived	
2-6-15 BUSSE BOOM	One truck load of stores arrived — including 6000 Respirators. D.O.O. visited Army H'd Q'rs	
3-6-15 BUSSE BOOM	Three Truck loads of stores arrived including 2 Water Carts and 33 loose Wheels. D.O.O. visited Army H'd Qrs	
4-6-15 POPERINGHE	Moves to POPERINGHE. One Truck load of stores arrived. Motor Car H/D.O.O. handed over to Div'l. Head Quarters —	

Army Form C. 2118.

WAR DIARY
or
INTELLIGENCE SUMMARY.

(Erase heading not required.)

Instructions regarding War Diaries and Intelligence Summaries are contained in F.S. Regs., Part II. and the Staff Manual respectively. Title pages will be prepared in manuscript.

Hour, Date, Place	Summary of Events and Information	Remarks and references to Appendices
5-6-15 POPERINGHE	One Truck load of Stores arrived	
6/6/15 POPERINGHE	Two Truck loads of Stores arrived including 2 Water Carts and 1 R.E. Tool Cart	
7/6/15 POPERINGHE	One truck load of Stores arrived.	
8/6/15 POPERINGHE	One truck load of Stores arrived	

Forms/C. 2118/10

WAR DIARY
or
INTELLIGENCE SUMMARY.
(Erase heading not required.)

Army Form C. 2118.

Hour, Date, Place	Summary of Events and Information	Remarks and references to Appendices
9/6/15 POPERINGHE	No stores arrived today. Issues and receipts normal.	
10/6/15 POPERINGHE	One truck load of stores arrived. Visit from Colonel EGAN and Major COURTICE	
11/6/15 POPERINGHE	No stores arrived today. Our Reserve Supply Wheats and Refrigerators fixed at 1 each Passengers and men. Demand forward for 14,000 of each to complete.	
12/6/15 POPERINGHE	2 Trucks stores arrived including Iron Shutters for Gas Alert.	
13/6/15 POPERINGHE	2 Trucks stores arrived including 2 Water Carts for G.S. Lorries, also 5050 Smoke Helmets	

Army Form C. 2118.

WAR DIARY
or
INTELLIGENCE SUMMARY.
(Erase heading not required.)

Instructions regarding War Diaries and Intelligence Summaries are contained in F.S. Regs., Part II. and the Staff Manual respectively. Title pages will be prepared in manuscript.

Hour, Date, Place	Summary of Events and Information	Remarks and references to Appendices
14-6-15 POPERINGHE	One Truck of Stores arrived including 4050 Smoke Helmets.	
15-6-15 POPERINGHE	One Truck of Stores arrived, including 8000 Respirators. No Motor Car available. Feb 11.30 am	
16-6-15 POPERINGHE	No stores arrived today. Appr got Canvas received from Ord S. Cap. Troth. Telegram late in day to say Stores had arrived at railhead - Sent lorries to collect.	
17-6-15 POPERINGHE	2 Truck loads Stores arrived including 2 Water Carts, 7000 Respirators and 1050 Smoke Helmets	
18-6-15 POPERINGHE	1 Truck stores arrived. Demands sent to France for 10 Machine Guns to replace losses. Considerable quantity of Rifles and Equipt. received from casualties.	

Forms/C. 2118/10

WAR DIARY
or
INTELLIGENCE SUMMARY.
(Erase heading not required.)

Army Form C. 2118.

Hour, Date, Place	Summary of Events and Information	Remarks and references to Appendices
19-6-15 POPERINGHE	Two truck loads stores arrived, including 5000 Rapid-gun and 2 Water Carts. Machine gun ammunition for 1 Mule.	
20-6-15 POPERINGHE	Unable to get Motor Car today during afternoon. Two Truck loads of stores arrived, including 2 Water Carts, 2 Machine guns. Machine guns demanded for 10th Inniskillings sent.	
21-6-15 POPERINGHE	Two Truck loads of stores arrived including 1 Water Cart and 10 Machine Guns. Stokes gun reports W. by 4th Middlesex. The gun recovered from enemy on 18th inst. repaired and issued.	
22-6-15 POPERINGHE	No stores arrived today. April to 19605 re inability to get Motor.	

Army Form C. 2118.

WAR DIARY
or
INTELLIGENCE SUMMARY.
(Erase heading not required.)

Instructions regarding War Diaries and Intelligence Summaries are contained in F. S. Regs., Part II. and the Staff Manual respectively. Title pages will be prepared in manuscript.

Hour, Date, Place	Summary of Events and Information	Remarks and references to Appendices
23-6-15 POPERINGHE	3 Machine Guns received today. 1 Truck load stores arrived	
24-6-15 POPERINGHE	2 Truck loads Stores arrived including one Water Cart and 5 Carriages Ambulance. 3900 Smoke Helmets received. 100 on leave	
25-6-15 POPERINGHE	2 Truck loads Stores arrived including 2 Ammn Wagons. 100 on leave	
26-6-15 POPERINGHE	1 Truck load of Stores arrived. 100 on leave	
27-6-15 POPERINGHE	1 Truck load of Stores arrived	

Army Form C. 2118.

WAR DIARY
or
INTELLIGENCE SUMMARY.

(Erase heading not required.)

Instructions regarding War Diaries and Intelligence Summaries are contained in F.S. Regs., Part II. and the Staff Manual respectively. Title pages will be prepared in manuscript.

Hour, Date, Place	Summary of Events and Information	Remarks and references to Appendices
28.6.15 POPERINGHE	One Truck arrived including 4650 South Helmets	
29.6.15 — " —	No stores arrived	
30.6.15 — " —	2 Trucks arrived including 3 Water carts. A.A.O.S. 3rd Army visited "dump"	

Arthur Myn
A.D.O.S. III Division

121/6272

3-48 /5 division

D.A.D.O.S. 8rd Division

Vol III

Army Form C. 2118.

WAR DIARY
~~INTELLIGENCE SUMMARY~~
(Erase heading not required.)

Confidential

War Diary of :-
D.A.D.O.S. 3rd Division.
(Major H.J. Bush
   a.o.o.)
From :- 1. 7. 15.
To :-   31. 7. 15.

Army Form C. 2118.

WAR DIARY
or
INTELLIGENCE SUMMARY.
(Erase heading not required.)

Instructions regarding War Diaries and Intelligence Summaries are contained in F.S. Regs., Part II. and the Staff Manual respectively. Title pages will be prepared in manuscript.

Hour, Date, Place		Summary of Events and Information	Remarks and references to Appendices
1-7-15	POPERINGHE	3 Trucks arrived including 3 Water Carts and 2 G.S. Wagons, also 1650 Smoke Helmets	
2-7-15	POPERINGHE	2 Trucks arrived including 1 Tool Cart and 1 body of Travelling Kitchen	
3-7-15	POPERINGHE	No stores arrived today	
4-7-15	POPERINGHE	1 Truck stores arrived today Direct from D.O.S.	
5-7-15	POPERINGHE	2 Trucks arrived including 1200 Smoke Helmets Visited D.D.O.S.	

Forms/C. 2118/10

Army Form C. 2118.

WAR DIARY
or
INTELLIGENCE SUMMARY.
(Erase heading not required.)

Instructions regarding War Diaries and Intelligence Summaries are contained in F.S. Regs, Part II. and the Staff Manual respectively. Title pages will be prepared in manuscript.

Hour, Date, Place	Summary of Events and Information	Remarks and references to Appendices
6-7-15 POPERINGHE	No stores arrived. Attained 1000 yards of Green Canvas from Army 4th D.S. Also some 4½ lbs of Acetone.	[3rd DIVISION stamp]
7-7-15 POPERINGHE	No stores arrived	[3rd DIVISION stamp]
8-7-15 POPERINGHE	3 Trucks arrived today including Water Cart for Royal Scots, — 6 Light Infantry 4 Machine Guns and 12000 Cap Centains fuses DDoS 2nd Army.	[3rd DIVISION stamp]
9-7-15 POPERINGHE	3 Trucks arrived including 4 Mens Carts and 1 Water Cart.	[3rd DIVISION stamp]
10-7-15 POPERINGHE	1 Truck arrived. 7000 Smoke Helmets received from 28th Division. 4 Machine Guns arrived 2 for Suffolks, 2 for Worcesters. Division now complete as regards Machine Guns, i.e. 4 per Battn.	[3rd DIVISION stamp]

WAR DIARY
or
INTELLIGENCE SUMMARY.

(Erase heading not required.)

Army Form C. 2118.

Hour, Date, Place	Summary of Events and Information	Remarks and references to Appendices
11-7-15 POPERINGHE	2 Trucks arrived including 1 Water Cart. Cycles Reached in afternoon to meet S.O.S. Rly. but did not arrive.	
12-7-15 POPERINGHE	1 Truck stores arrived today.	
13-7-15 POPERINGHE	3 Trucks arrived including 50 Bicycles, 1 G.S. Wagon, 1 Mess Cart, one 18 pounder Gun and Carriage, and 38 Vermorel Sprayers.	
14-7-15 POPERINGHE	No stores today. Visited D.A.D.O.S. Army H.Q.	
15-7-15 POPERINGHE	2 Trucks arrived including 6 Sprayers and 450 Smoke Helmets.	
16-7-15 POPERINGHE	2 Trucks arrived including 1 Limbered Wagon for Supplies Train. S.S. 11th arrived for course of Instruction.	

Army Form C. 2118.

WAR DIARY
or
INTELLIGENCE SUMMARY.
(Erase heading not required.)

Instructions regarding War Diaries and Intelligence Summaries are contained in F.S. Regs., Part II. and the Staff Manual respectively. Title pages will be prepared in manuscript.

Hour, Date, Place		Summary of Events and Information	Remarks and references to Appendices
14.7.15	POPERINGHE	1 Truck stores arrived. Sgt Hamley left for 2nd Division for duty.	
15.7.15	POPERINGHE	1 Truck stores arrived, including 494 Smoke Helmets	
19.7.15	POPERINGHE	1 Truck stores arrived including 2126 Smoke Helmets	
20.7.15	POPERINGHE	1 Truck stores arrived including 2000 Smoke Helmets	
21.7.15	POPERINGHE	No stores arrived. Pte Ford joined for duty from base	
22.7.15	POPERINGHE	1 Truck stores arrived. 2 Machine Guns demanded for 1st Middlesex Regt. Unable to get Motor Car today	

Form C. 2118/10

Army Form C. 2118.

WAR DIARY
or
INTELLIGENCE SUMMARY.
(Erase heading not required.)

Instructions regarding War Diaries and Intelligence Summaries are contained in F.S. Regs., Part II. and the Staff Manual respectively. Title pages will be prepared in manuscript.

Hour, Date, Place	Summary of Events and Information	Remarks and references to Appendices
23-7-15 POPERINGHE	2 Trucks arrived including 9000 Smoke Helmets and 3 Water Carts. 2875 Smoke Helmets issued to 17th Div. Maxim Gun demanded for 1st Jackson Herts Forces 2nd army	
24-7-15 POPERINGHE	1 Truck arrived	
25-7-15 Poperinghe	1 Truck arrived including 6313 Smoke Helmets. 2 Maxim Guns for 4 Cheshires Regt. Received 6313 Smoke helmets from Dare.	
26-7-15 Poperinghe	1 Truck arrived including Alarm Gun for 1/Gordons. 9 Water Carts for 9th y/s D.C.L.I. Received 2600 Smoke helmets from Dare.	

Army Form C. 2118.

WAR DIARY
or
INTELLIGENCE SUMMARY.
(Erase heading not required.)

Instructions regarding War Diaries and Intelligence Summaries are contained in F.S. Regs., Part II. and the Staff Manual respectively. Title pages will be prepared in manuscript.

Hour, Date, Place	Summary of Events and Information	Remarks and references to Appendices
27.7.15 POPERINGHE	No stores arrived to day.	
28.7.15 Poperinghe	No Stores arrived	
29.7.15 Poperinghe	1 Truck of Stores Arrived. Moved dump to Farden 1 mile N.W. of RENINGHELST.	
30.7.15 Reninghelst	No Stores Arrived	
31.7.15 RENINGHELST	1 Truck Stores arrived including 6500 Smoke Helmets. Reserve of 1 Smoke Helmet per man now complete.	

Forms/C. 2118/10

3rd Division DADOS

Confidential

War Diary
of

D.A.D.O.S. III Division

from 1st to 31st Augt 1915

Vol IV

121/6598

Army Form C. 2118.

WAR DIARY
or
INTELLIGENCE SUMMARY.
(Erase heading not required.)

Instructions regarding War Diaries and Intelligence Summaries are contained in F.S. Regs., Part II. and the Staff Manual respectively. Title pages will be prepared in manuscript.

Hour, Date, Place	Summary of Events and Information	Remarks and references to Appendices
1-8-15 RENINGHELST	No stores today - No Car available in afternoon.	
2-8-15 RENINGHELST	1 Truck stores arrived including 2000 Packets for Smoke Helmets. All Packets now received. Visited D.D.O.S. 2nd Army.	
3-8-15 RENINGHELST	1 Truck stores arrived. S.Sgt Hall left for Home.	
4-8-15 RENINGHELST	1 Truck stores arrived today including 1580 Smoke Helmets and 870 prs Boots	
5-8-15 RENINGHELST	1 Truck stores arrived - Visited DDOS 2nd Army	
6-8-15 RENINGHELST	1 Truck stores arrived	

Forms/C. 2118/10

Army Form C. 2118

WAR DIARY
or
INTELLIGENCE SUMMARY.
(Erase heading not required.)

Instructions regarding War Diaries and Intelligence Summaries are contained in F.S. Regs., Part II. and the Staff Manual respectively. Title pages will be prepared in manuscript.

Hour, Date, Place	Summary of Events and Information	Remarks and references to Appendices
7.8.15 RENINGHELST	1 Truck arrived including 2 G.S. Wagons and 1500 Smoke Helmets	[stamp] D.O.O. 3rd DIVISION
8.9.15 RENINGHELST	1 Truck arrived	[stamp] D.O.O. 3rd DIVISION
9.8.15 RENINGHELST	1 Truck arrived	[stamp] D.O.O. 3rd DIVISION
10.8.15 RENINGHELST	1 Truck arrived. 20 Shaped Steel Helmets and 150 Rockets taken over from 5th Corps	[stamp] D.O.O. 3rd DIVISION
11.8.15 RENINGHELST	1 Truck arrived	[stamp] D.O.O. 3rd DIVISION
12.8.15 RENINGHELST	1 Truck arrived including 1000 Smoke Helmets taken over from 2nd Army	[stamp] D.O.O. 3rd DIVISION

Army Form C. 2118

WAR DIARY
or
INTELLIGENCE SUMMARY.
(Erase heading not required.)

Instructions regarding War Diaries and Intelligence Summaries are contained in F. S. Regs., Part II. and the Staff Manual respectively. Title pages will be prepared in manuscript.

Hour, Date, Place	Summary of Events and Information	Remarks and references to Appendices
13/8/15 RENINGHELST.	2 Truck arrived including 20860 Smoke Helmets (2nd issue). This completes to 2 per man 18 pdr gun team for 109th Bty and 1 per man in reserve	[D.O.O. 3rd Division stamp]
14/8/15 RENINGHELST	1 Truck arrived including 6440 Tube pattern Smoke Helmets. Issue of 2nd Helmet for Officers and men were completed	[D.O.O. 3rd Division stamp]
15/8/15 RENINGHELST.	1 Truck arrived. Maxim gun ammunition for H.T.C.	[D.O.O. 3rd Division stamp]
16/8/15 RENINGHELST	18 pdr gun arrived for 109th Battery. 1 Truck stores arrived. Machine gun for H.T.C. arrived from Calais by Motor Convoy.	[D.O.O. 3rd Division stamp]
17/8/15 RENINGHELST.	No stores today. 2 Trench Mortars received from O.O. 5th Corps.	[D.O.O. 3rd Division stamp]

Forms/C. 2118/10

Army Form C. 2118.

WAR DIARY
or
INTELLIGENCE SUMMARY.
(Erase heading not required.)

Instructions regarding War Diaries and Intelligence Summaries are contained in F.S. Regs., Part II. and the Staff Manual respectively. Title pages will be prepared in manuscript.

Hour, Date, Place	Summary of Events and Information	Remarks and references to Appendices
RENINGHELST 19/8/15	1 Truck Stores arrived	
RENINGHELST 19/8/15	1 Truck stores arrived. 7863 Pte Pinder joined in relief of Pte Ford.	
RENINGHELST 20/8/15	Pte Ford left for Home. 2 Trucks arrived including 2 rear portions of Limbered Wagons for Worcesters.	
RENINGHELST 21/8/15	2 Trucks arrived including Water Cart for 41st Bty.	
RENINGHELST 22/8/15	2 Trucks arrived including 1 G.S. Wagon for Divn Train. 1334 Satchels and 3500 Tube pattern Smoke Helmets. The Tube pattern Helmets have been issued to 8th and 14th Divn 1750 each	
RENINGHELST 23/8/15	1 Truck stores arrived. Visited D.A.D.O.S. 2nd Army	

Forms/C. 2118/10

Army Form C. 2118.

WAR DIARY
or
INTELLIGENCE SUMMARY.
(Erase heading not required.)

Hour, Date, Place	Summary of Events and Information	Remarks and references to Appendices
24-8-15 RENINGHELST	1 Truck arrived with Lumber, G.S. Wagon for Ifordens and 1st Royal Scots Fus. and Maltese Cart for 7/M.3.	[stamps: D.A.O. 3rd DIVISION]
25-8-15 RENINGHELST	1 Truck arrived today. 2408 Tube Pattern Helmets received from 3rd Div. and 1225 from 17th Div.	
26-8-15 RENINGHELST	3 Trucks arrived including Lumbered Wagon for 56 Coy R.E. and Amm Wagon and Limber for 40 MFO.	
27-8-15 RENINGHELST	2 Trucks arrived including G.S. Wagon for Div Train and tube pattern of Lumbered Wagon, 2000 Tube Pattern Helmets received from Ord S. Corps	
28-8-15 RENINGHELST	1 Truck arrived	
29-8-15 RENINGHELST	1 Truck arrived including 1190 Smoke Helmets Tube Pattern	

Army Form C. 2118.

WAR DIARY
or
INTELLIGENCE SUMMARY.
(Erase heading not required.)

Instructions regarding War Diaries and Intelligence Summaries are contained in F.S. Regs., Part II. and the Staff Manual respectively. Title pages will be prepared in manuscript.

Hour, Date, Place	Summary of Events and Information	Remarks and references to Appendices
30-8-15 RENINGHELST	1 Truck stores arrived also 4 Mess Carts 8190 Tube pattern Helmets received from Base Depôt & 190 from 6th Div.	
31-8-15 RENINGHELST	1 Truck arrived. Visited 10,100 S. 2nd Army	

J Monro Major
19 KRRC
III Division
1/9/15

3rd Division
bros

Confidential

121/6902

War Diary
of
DADOS 3rd Divn
(Lt. Col. H.S. Bush)
AOD

from 1/9/15 to 30/9/15

Vol V

Army Form C. 2118

WAR DIARY
or
INTELLIGENCE SUMMARY.
(Erase heading not required.)

Instructions regarding War Diaries and Intelligence Summaries are contained in F. S. Regs., Part II. and the Staff Manual respectively. Title pages will be prepared in manuscript.

Hour, Date, Place	Summary of Events and Information	Remarks and references to Appendices
30-8-15 RENINGHELST	1 Truck Supply Stores arrived also 4 Mess Carts. 8.20 Tube Helmets received from Base and 4190 from 6th Division	
31-8-15 RENINGHELST	1 Truck arrived. No les D.D.O.S. 2nd Army.	
1-9-15 RENINGHELST	2 Trucks arrived including 1 Mess Cart and 1 potato masher also kitchen fan for H.A.C. to replace German fan. Major	
2/9/15 RENINGHELST	2 Trucks arrived including 2 Horse/Pulling Limbered Wagons	
3/9/15 RENINGHELST	1 Truck arrived - Horse Shoes and 1000 Suitable Inner Helmets	
4/9/15 RENINGHELST	1 Truck arrived including 4375 Fringes Brabant which have been due from Base since 13/6/15	

(9.29.6) W 4141-463 100,000 9/14 H W V Forms/C. 2118/10

Army Form C. 2118.

WAR DIARY
or
INTELLIGENCE SUMMARY.
(Erase heading not required.)

Instructions regarding War Diaries and Intelligence Summaries are contained in F.S. Regs., Part II. and the Staff Manual respectively. Title pages will be prepared in manuscript.

Hour, Date, Place	Summary of Events and Information	Remarks and references to Appendices
6-9-15 RENINGHELST	2 Trucks arrived including 200 C.S. Tents and 2 G.S. Limbered Wagons for Cheshire R.E.	
7-9-15 RENINGHELST	1 Truck arrived including 2600 Blankets	
8-9-15 RENINGHELST	2 Trucks arrived including 2750 Blankets and Water Cart for 1 M.F.	
9-9-15 RENINGHELST	3 Trucks arrived including 3190 Blankets	
11-9-15 RENINGHELST	2 Trucks arrived including 2 G.S. Wagons for 10in Trench 30 Illuminating Pistols and 1168 Satchels	
11-9-15 RENINGHELST	1 Truck stores arrived	

Forms/C. 2118/10

Army Form C. 2118.

WAR DIARY
or
INTELLIGENCE SUMMARY.
(Erase heading not required.)

Instructions regarding War Diaries and Intelligence Summaries are contained in F. S. Regs., Part II. and the Staff Manual respectively. Title pages will be prepared in manuscript.

Hour, Date, Place		Summary of Events and Information	Remarks and references to Appendices
12-9-15	PENINGHELST	2 Trucks arrived. 7000 Satchels for Helmets, 18pr June for 109th Battery, 3000 Blankets, etc.	[stamp] 3rd DIVISION D.O.O.
13-9-15	RENINGHELST	1 Truck arrived	[stamp] 3rd DIVISION D.O.O.
14-9-15	RENINGHELST	No stores arrived with exception of 2 Water Carts. No Motor Car available.	[stamp] 3rd DIVISION D.O.O.
15-9-15	RENINGHELST	1 Truck & tires arrived including 850pr Boots, and 7000 Satchels for Tube Helmets. No Motor Car available in morning.	[stamp] 3rd DIVISION D.O.O.
16-9-15	RENINGHELST	2 Trucks arrived including 1 G.S. Wagon and 3398 Smoke Satchels Helmets	[stamp] 3rd DIVISION D.O.O.
17-9-15	PENINGHELST	3 Trucks arrived including 47 Soyers Stoves, 106 Primus Horse Shoes, 400 pr Gum Boots and 1 Gun Carriage for 109th Battery	[stamp] 3rd DIVISION D.O.O.

Forms/C. 2118/10

Army Form C. 2118

WAR DIARY
or
INTELLIGENCE SUMMARY.
(Erase heading not required.)

Instructions regarding War Diaries and Intelligence Summaries are contained in F.S. Regs., Part II. and the Staff Manual respectively. Title pages will be prepared in manuscript.

Hour, Date, Place	Summary of Events and Information	Remarks and references to Appendices
18-9-15 RENINGHELST	8 Trucks arrived including 600 Lahore tickets, 100 Tents and Trench Clothing	
19-9-15 RENINGHELST	9 Trucks including 120 Tents and 3 Mess Carts	
20-9-15 RENINGHELST	3 Trucks arrived including 1. G.S. Limbered Wagon (for fusion) and 2 Mess Carts for Genl Staff. Postes Calais for Store for General Staff	
21-9-15 RENINGHELST	2 Trucks arrived including 1 Water Cart and 1 Machine Gun for "R" Scots Fus. Postes Boulogne for Stores for General Staff	
22-9-15 RENINGHELST	2 Trucks arrived today including 1 Mallow Cart 3 L 71.9 Passivatus and 995 for Boots	
25-9-15 RENINGHELST	3 Trucks arrived including 1 Trav. Kitchen 3 Water Carts 1 G.S. Limbered Wagon	

Forms/C. 2118/10

Army Form C. 2118.

WAR DIARY
or
INTELLIGENCE SUMMARY.
(Erase heading not required.)

Instructions regarding War Diaries and Intelligence Summaries are contained in F.S. Regs., Part II. and the Staff Manual respectively. Title pages will be prepared in manuscript.

Hour, Date, Place	Summary of Events and Information	Remarks and references to Appendices
24-9-15 RENINGHELST	2 Trucks arrived including Bulk Horse Stores and 1 pair of Limbered Wagon for 1/Kensingtons, also 100 Night Sights	[stamps]
25-9-15 RENINGHELST	8 Trucks arrived including 2 Gun Carriages & Matériel and Bulk Clothing, 1500 Tube Helmets obtained from 5th Corps.	
26-9-15 RENINGHELST	1 Truck stores arrived including Bulk Stores Ind 5 ohm, 200 Verys Pistols and 11 Catapults, and 36 Jelures 936.	
27-9-15 RENINGHELST	2 Truck stores arrived including 310 H. Lamps and 2 G.S. Limbered Wagons	
28-9-15 RENINGHELST	No Ordnance Stores today. 2 Truck Loads furniture and Stores for Y.M.C.A. obtained by A.O.10.	
29-9-15 RENINGHELST	3 Trucks arrived including 5 Machine Guns 3 Tripods complete, and 1 Trench Kitchen Boiler for 3/Worcesters	

Army Form C. 2118.

WAR DIARY
or
INTELLIGENCE SUMMARY.
(Erase heading not required.)

Instructions regarding War Diaries and Intelligence Summaries are contained in F.S. Regs., Part II. and the Staff Manual respectively. Title pages will be prepared in manuscript.

Hour, Date, Place	Summary of Events and Information	Remarks and references to Appendices
30-9-15 ARMENTIERES	2 Trucks arrived including 2 Limbers 9 G.S. Wagons and 1 Motor Cart for 75 Guns and 1 third portion of Limbered Wagon for 172 Tunnellers also 1500 Satchels for Tube Helmets.	[stamp: D.A.D.O.S. 3rd DIVISION]
	3rd Division 30/9/15	J. Moreland Lt Col DAD OS

3rd Division

Confidential

War Diary   121/7599

of

D.A.D.O.S 3rd Division

from 1-10-15 to 31-10-15

Vol VI

Army Form C. 2118.

WAR DIARY
or
INTELLIGENCE SUMMARY.
(Erase heading not required.)

Instructions regarding War Diaries and Intelligence Summaries are contained in F. S. Regs., Part II. and the Staff Manual respectively. Title pages will be prepared in manuscript.

Hour, Date, Place	Summary of Events and Information	Remarks and references to Appendices
1-10-15 RENINGHELST	1 Truck arrived including Bulk Horse Shoes and 360 night Sights	
2-10-15 RENINGHELST	2 Trucks arrived including 2 Hind Rations G.S. Limbers Wagons for 1/n.7.	
3-10-15 RENINGHELST	1 Truck stores arrived inclusion Drill finishing gun	
4-10-15 RENINGHELST	2 Trucks arrived including 1 G.S. Wagon for 29th Battery	
5-10-15 RENINGHELST	No stores today	

Army Form C. 2118.

WAR DIARY
or
INTELLIGENCE SUMMARY.
(Erase heading not required.)

Instructions regarding War Diaries and Intelligence Summaries are contained in F.S. Regs., Part II. and the Staff Manual respectively. Title pages will be prepared in manuscript.

Hour, Date, Place	Summary of Events and Information	Remarks and references to Appendices
6-10-15 RENINGHELST	3 Trucks arrived including 200 Tents and 100 Tents D'avril Hangars, also 3 third pattern of G.S. Limbers Wagons for 2/Rif Scots	
7-10-15 RENINGHELST	2 Trucks arrived including 1 Carriage & 5" Howitzer 129th By and 2 Wagons Amn 18 pdr 23rd Fd Bde R.F.A.	
8-10-15 RENINGHELST	2 Trucks arrived including 100 Tents, Bulk Horse Shoes and 3 Machine Guns for H/Machine Guns and 1 Machine Gun for 2/RS Fus. 2000 Tube helmets from 2nd Corps	
9-10-15 RENINGHELST	2 Trucks arrived including 1 STFF. Cart for 2/Suffolks Bulk S.A.A. Clothing, and 2000 Satchels	
10-10-15 RENINGHELST	2 Trucks arrived including Bulk picketing gear and 45 Bicycles	
11-10-15 RENINGHELST	2 Trucks arrived including 1640 Drawers Woollen and Vests H.Qs 2nd Army Bulk Shirts Socks and Towels.	

Forms/C. 2118/10

Army Form C. 2118.

WAR DIARY
or
INTELLIGENCE SUMMARY.
(Erase heading not required.)

Instructions regarding War Diaries and Intelligence Summaries are contained in F.S. Regs., Part II. and the Staff Manual respectively. Title pages will be prepared in manuscript.

Hour, Date, Place		Summary of Events and Information	Remarks and references to Appendices
RENINGHELST	12-10-15	2 Trucks arrived including 1 G.S. Wagon for 3/1 Div Train and 1 Mess Cart for 1/Londons	[stamp: D.O.O. 3rd DIVISION]
RENINGHELST	13-10-15	1 Truck Stores including 730 prs Boots and 4000 pr Laces	[stamp: D.O.O. 3rd DIVISION]
RENINGHELST	14-10-15	1 Truck Stores arrived including Bulk Soap, Oil of grease etc 600 prs Boots from Regt received from OR 5th Cycles Coys	[stamp: D.O.O. 3rd DIVISION]
RENINGHELST	15-10-15	1 Truck arrived including 104 Brown Horse Shoes and 11 Very Pistols, 10 Mell Fees and 9 Shafts LA issued from 25 Rly	[stamp: D.O.O. 3rd DIVISION]
RENINGHELST	16-10-15	2 Trucks arrived including Bulk Clothing and 1 G.S. Limbered Wagon for H.A.C., also 200 Trench Helmets 2/S Lancs, 3/Worcesters, 1/Wilts and 2/R.I.R. to conform to 25th Div	[stamp: D.O.O. 3rd DIVISION]
RENINGHELST	17-10-15	1 Truck arrived including Bulk Petroleum from No. 07284 Sgt Forty P.W. arrived for instruction on 3rd M.O. O. 44681 L/Cpl Statham T.A. arrived for duty " 06334 2/Cpl Brown F " " " 07759 1/Pte Cooper S.J. " "	[stamp: D.O.O. 3rd DIVISION]

Form C. 2118/10

(29 6) W 4141—463 100,000 9/14 H W V

Army Form C. 2118.

WAR DIARY
or
INTELLIGENCE SUMMARY.
(Erase heading not required.)

Instructions regarding War Diaries and Intelligence Summaries are contained in F.S. Regs., Part II. and the Staff Manual respectively. Title pages will be prepared in manuscript.

Hour, Date, Place	Summary of Events and Information	Remarks and references to Appendices
18-10-15 RENINGHELST	2 Trucks arrived including 1 Motor Cart for 2/Rifles and 1 Mother Cart for 2/R Scots, also Maxim fittings for 10th Lincoln Sets	
19-10-15 RENINGHELST	1 G.S. Limber Wagon arrived for 110th Section Two. No other stores	
20-10-15 RENINGHELST	1 Truck arrived including Boots and spare Cylinders for Breathing Sets	
21-10-15 RENINGHELST	1 Truck stores arrived including 1 cwt Oil, Rubber, Soap &c.	
22-10-15 RENINGHELST	1 Truck arrived including Bulk Horse Shoes. Moved to Steenvoorde. 0.6978 Pte C. Smade } Left for Boulogne en route to Woolwich 0.6192 " A. Adams } 0.6865 " H. Purton }	
23-10-15 STEENVOORDE	3 Trucks arrived including 6000 Zinc Woodworks	

Forms/C. 2118/10

Army Form C. 2118.

WAR DIARY
or
INTELLIGENCE SUMMARY.
(Erase heading not required.)

Instructions regarding War Diaries and Intelligence Summaries are contained in F. S. Regs., Part II. and the Staff Manual respectively. Title pages will be prepared in manuscript.

Hour, Date, Place	Summary of Events and Information	Remarks and references to Appendices
24-10-15 Steenvoorde	1 Truck arrived today including 335 Wagoners for Infantry. 700 Brazier and 3000 Cattles for Smoke Helmets	[stamp]
25-10-15 Steenvoorde	1 Truck arrived including Bulk Shirts Socks Towels &c, also 11 Very Pistols and 2 Miller James Statters	[stamp]
26-10-15 Steenvoorde	No stores today	[stamp]
27-10-15 Steenvoorde	1 Truck stores today including 400 Boots	[stamp]
28-10-15 STEENVOORDE	1 Truck arrived including Bulk Mess Tins, Watchbottles, Oil, Rubbing Grease &c. Sergt Jordy left for 27th Division	[stamp]

Army Form C. 2118.

WAR DIARY
or
INTELLIGENCE SUMMARY.
(Erase heading not required.)

Instructions regarding War Diaries and Intelligence Summaries are contained in F.S. Regs., Part II. and the Staff Manual respectively. Title pages will be prepared in manuscript.

Hour, Date, Place	Summary of Events and Information	Remarks and references to Appendices
29-10-15. STEENVOORDE	8 Trucks arrived, including 9900 Capes Mackintosh and 20,000 Soles Inner Ankle Boots, also Boots Shoes, Shirts and 6 Tarpaulins	
30-10-15. STEENVOORDE	6 Trucks arrived to day, including 6000 Horse Rugs 1000 prs Gum Boots Thigh, 3000 Shirts 6000 Drawers 3000 Socks and Bulk Clothing. All Trucks cleared 1 Water Cart for 130th Battery by 4 p.m.	
31-10-15 STEENVOORDE	1 Truck arrived including Bulk Picketing Gear. Major Courtice erected Depot	

B Murison Capt
I.D.A.D.O.S.
3rd Division

3rd Division

Confidential

121/7637

War Diary

of

D.A.D.V.S. 3rd Div

from 29-10-15 to 30-11-15

Vol VII

Army Form C. 2118.

WAR DIARY
or
INTELLIGENCE SUMMARY.
(Erase heading not required.)

Instructions regarding War Diaries and Intelligence Summaries are contained in F.S. Regs., Part II. and the Staff Manual respectively. Title pages will be prepared in manuscript.

Hour, Date, Place	Summary of Events and Information	Remarks and references to Appendices
29-10-15 STEENVOORDE	3 Trucks arrived including 9900 Capes Mackintosh and 30000 Soles inner Ankle Boots, also Bulk Horse Shoes and 6 Tarpaulins	
30-10-15 STEENVOORDE	6 Trucks arrived today including 6000 Horse Rugs 1000 pr Fur Boots Thigh, 3000 Shirts, 6000 Drawers 30000 Socks and Bulk Clothing. All Trucks cleared 1 Water Cart for 130th Battery by 4 pm.	
31-10-15 STEENVOORDE	1 Truck arrived including Bulk Pickelhaubes Major Coutha viates Rifles	
1-11-15 STEENVOORDE	2 Trucks arrived including Bulk Shirts Soap 84, and 2 G.S. Wagons for H.Q. 3rd Phis Train, also Tent Nails	
2-11-15 STEENVOORDE	2 Trucks arrived including 700 Boots F.S. and 1 Water Cart for 1st Suffolks	

Army Form C. 2118.

WAR DIARY
or
INTELLIGENCE SUMMARY.
(Erase heading not required.)

Instructions regarding War Diaries and Intelligence Summaries are contained in F.S. Regs., Part II. and the Staff Manual respectively. Title pages will be prepared in manuscript.

Hour, Date, Place	Summary of Events and Information	Remarks and references to Appendices
3-11-15 STEENVOORDE	2 Trucks arrived including Bulk Boots and 600 Leather Baskets	[stamp: D.A.Q. 3rd Division]
4-11-15 STEENVOORDE	1 Truck arrived including Bulk Oil, Soap, Rations &c.	[stamp: D.A.Q. 3rd Division]
5-11-15 STEENVOORDE	1 Truck arrived including Bulk Horse Shoes and 1000 Satchels for Smoke Helmets	[stamp: D.A.Q. 3rd Division]
6-11-15 STEENVOORDE	1 Truck arrived including Bulk Clothing and 346 Steel Trench Helmets	[stamp: D.A.Q. 3rd Division]
7-11-15 STEENVOORDE	2 Trucks arrived including Bulk Jerreed Straw and 1000 Boots Gum Thigh	[stamp: D.A.Q. 3rd Division]

Army Form C. 2118.

WAR DIARY
or
INTELLIGENCE SUMMARY.
(Erase heading not required.)

Instructions regarding War Diaries and Intelligence Summaries are contained in F.S. Regs., Part II. and the Staff Manual respectively. Title pages will be prepared in manuscript.

Hour, Date, Place	Summary of Events and Information	Remarks and references to Appendices
8-11-15 STEENVOORDE	2 Trucks arrived containing Bulk Clothing and 4200 Leather Jerkins and 1020 Undercoats Fur.	
9-11-15 STEENVOORDE	Lieut Bearf joined for duty from 1st Corps Railhead. 1 Truck arrived containing 1 Maltese Cart for 1st DAC and 1 G.S. Limbered Wagon for 4th R.Fus.	
10-11-15 STEENVOORDE	2 Trucks arrived including 700 pair Boots, 728 pairs Boots Jum Thigh, 2 Wheeled Stretchers, 14 Shield Entrenching and 30 Salveus breathing Sets.	
11-11-15 STEENVOORDE	2 Trucks arrived including Bulk General Stores, 3 Marquees and 1 Mule Cart for 4 R Fusiliers.	
12-11-15 STEENVOORDE	2 Trucks arrived including 30000 pairs Jersey, 10000 Body Belts and 2310 Capes Waterproof, also bulk Horse Stores.	

Forms/C. 2118/10

Army Form C. 2118.

WAR DIARY
or
INTELLIGENCE SUMMARY.
(Erase heading not required.)

Instructions regarding War Diaries and Intelligence Summaries are contained in F. S. Regs., Part II. and the Staff Manual respectively. Title pages will be prepared in manuscript.

Hour, Date, Place	Summary of Events and Information	Remarks and references to Appendices
13-11-15 STEENVOORDE	1 Truck arrived including Bulk Clothing	
14-11-15 STEENVOORDE	1 Truck arrived including Bulk Pakthysson and 940 pr Boots, also 50 Horse Clippers	
15/11/15 STEENVOORDE	2 Trucks including Bulk Shirts, Socks etc, and 1 G.S. Wagon for 2 Coy 3rd Div Train. Visit from Col. Heron and Col Hale	
16-11-15 STEENVOORDE	1 Truck arrived including 1500 Leather Jerkins	
17-11-15 STEENVOORDE	2 Trucks arrived including 770 prs Boots and 6 sets Ward Marquee Bottoms, 3 Sets Bottoms sent on to 17th Div	

Army Form C. 2118.

WAR DIARY
or
INTELLIGENCE SUMMARY.
(Erase heading not required.)

Instructions regarding War Diaries and Intelligence Summaries are contained in F.S. Regs., Part II. and the Staff Manual respectively. Title pages will be prepared in manuscript.

Hour, Date, Place	Summary of Events and Information	Remarks and references to Appendices
STEENVOORDE 18-11-15	1 Truck arrived today including Bulk general stores 300 jerkins, 1000 Satchels for Tube Helmets	
STEENVOORDE 19-11-15	1 Truck stores including Horse Shoes and 89 Magazines for Lewis Guns	
STEENVOORDE 20-11-15	2 Trucks arrived including Bulk Clothing and 1 Body of Travelling Kitchen for 19th West Yorks.	
STEENVOORDE 21-11-15	1 Truck arrived including Bulk general stores and 800 prs of Boots	
RENINGHELST 22-11-15	1 Truck arrived including bulk Shirts, Socks &c, 180 Magazines for Lewis Guns, Tent Nails, Tapes and Wrenches	

Forms/C. 2118/10

Army Form C. 2118.

WAR DIARY
or
INTELLIGENCE SUMMARY.
(Erase heading not required.)

Instructions regarding War Diaries and Intelligence Summaries are contained in F. S. Regs., Part II. and the Staff Manual respectively. Title pages will be prepared in manuscript.

Hour, Date, Place	Summary of Events and Information	Remarks and references to Appendices
23-11-15 RENINGHELST	1 Truck stores including 2100 Waistcoats fur and 5000 Gloves fingerless	MS
24-11-15 RENINGHELST	2 Trucks including 150 Tents C.S.L. and 1180 pairs Boots also 12 Bicycles	MS
25-11-15 RENINGHELST	1 Truck stores including bulk Soap, Oil &c, and 21 Bicycles	MS
26-11-15 RENINGHELST	3 Trucks today including 11280 Tube Helmets, 4000 Fingerless Gloves and Bulk Horse Shoes	MS
27-11-15 RENINGHELST	7 Truck stores including 50 Sabours, 10000 Blankets, 1000 Vests, 150 Sweaters, 300 Brazier, Bulk S.D. Clothing and 1 Travelling Kitchen for 2/Suffolks - 5 lorries borrowed from Army Hd Qrs. for conveyance of stores.	MS

Forms/C. 2118/10

Army Form C. 2118

WAR DIARY
or
INTELLIGENCE SUMMARY
(Erase heading not required.)

Instructions regarding War Diaries and Intelligence Summaries are contained in F. S. Regs., Part II. and the Staff Manual respectively. Title Pages will be prepared in manuscript.

Place	Date	Hour	Summary of Events and Information	Remarks and references to Appendices
RENINGHELST	28/11/15		3 Trucks arrived today including 10,200 Tube Helmets, General Stores	
RENINGHELST	29/11/15		4 Trucks arrived including 10,000 Brassards, 3,000 Shirts, 8,100 Socks, 3,000 Towels, 4,000 Goggles, 520 Tube Helmets, 1 Lewis Machine gun, 150 Magazines for Lewis Gun etc. Visited D.D.O.S. 2nd Army.	
RENINGHELST	30/11/15		No stores from Base. 1,000 pr Boots from Thigh from 5th Corps	

J Smith Lt Col
D.A.D.O.S
3rd Div

D.D.O.S. 3º Sion.

Dag
vol VIII

Army Form C. 2118.

WAR DIARY
or
INTELLIGENCE SUMMARY

(Erase heading not required.)

Instructions regarding War Diaries and Intelligence Summaries are contained in F.S. Regs., Part II. and the Staff Manual respectively. Title Pages will be prepared in manuscript.

Place	Date	Hour	Summary of Events and Information	Remarks and references to Appendices
RENINGHELST	1/12/15		1 Truck stores arrived including 1555 prs Boots, 1540 Leather Jerkins, 10 Vermorel Sprayers, etc.	
RENINGHELST	2/12/15		1 Truck stores arrived including Bulk Oil, Soap, Rubbing &c.	
RENINGHELST	3/12/15		2 Trucks arrived including 50 Sail Covers for Huts, Bulk Horse Stores, 11 Cataphotes	
RENINGHELST	4/12/15		1 Truck stores including Bulk Clothing	
RENINGHELST	5/12/15		2 Trucks arrived including Bulk Picketing Gear and 12,000 Studs in lieu of Vests	

1875 Wt. W593/826 1,000,000 4/15 J.B.C. & A. A.D.S.S./Forms/C. 2118.

Army Form C. 2118

WAR DIARY
or
INTELLIGENCE SUMMARY
(Erase heading not required.)

Instructions regarding War Diaries and Intelligence Summaries are contained in F. S. Regs., Part II. and the Staff Manual respectively. Title Pages will be prepared in manuscript.

Place	Date	Hour	Summary of Events and Information	Remarks and references to Appendices
RENINGHELST	6/12/15		3 Trucks arrived including 1 G.S. Limbered Wagon for 12th West Yorks, 1 Rations Wagon for Chaplin Coy R.E. 1000 Shirts &c.	
RENINGHELST	7/12/15		1 Truck arrived today including 52 Boxes Horse Shoes, 3 Periscopes 71M, Wrenches and Tops for Steel Caps. 1500 prs Jew Boots High from Stores	
RENINGHELST	8/12/15		3 Trucks arrived enclosing 1865 prs Boots	
RENINGHELST	9/12/15		2 Trucks arrived including Bulk Soap, Oil Washing &c, 400 Capes Waterproof. 200 lbs Cable &c for Tents. 8000 Shirts. 500 Undercoats Fur. 8100 Socks	
RENINGHELST	10/12/15		1 Truck arrived including 142 Boxes Horse Shoes and 15 Cases Mule Shoes. Visited 1 R.F. 9/5 2nd Army re Machine Guns	

1875. Wt. W593/826 1,000,000 4/15 J.B.C. & A. A.D.S.S./Forms/C. 2118.

Army Form C. 2118

WAR DIARY
or
INTELLIGENCE SUMMARY
(Erase heading not required.)

Instructions regarding War Diaries and Intelligence Summaries are contained in F.S. Regs., Part II. and the Staff Manual respectively. Title Pages will be prepared in manuscript.

Place	Date	Hour	Summary of Events and Information	Remarks and references to Appendices
RENINGHELST	11-12-15		3 Trucks arrived including 3 Water Carts and 4 G.S. Limbered Wagons for M.G.C. Bulk Clothing including 14,3000 Goggles and 300 Magazines for Lewis Guns	M.S.
PENINGHELST	12/12/15		2 Trucks arrived including Bulk Picketing Gear, 193 Limbered Wagons M.G. Corps and 1 Water Cart for 2/R Scots. No 0838 Sgt Watts arrived for instruction as Bde W.O.	M.S.
PENINGHELST	13/12/15		1 Truck arrived including Bulk Woollen Socks, Towels, Caps, 69 Boxes Horseshoes and 1700 pr goggles	M.S.
RENINGHELST	14/12/15		No stores today. 1000 Smoke Helmets and 50 Rifle Muzzle Protectors	M.S.
RENINGHELST	15/12/15		1 Truck today including 1000 Caps Waisted, 2500 pr drawers Woollen, 570 pr Boots, Ans tr No 14 Peninopes. Also the 6 Sets Harness for 3 Limbered G.S. Wagons	M.S.

O. 6297 L/Cpl Connell Acth
O. 9590 Pte Coles   G.W. Arrived for duty
O. 7532 " Davies   a.

Army Form C. 2118

WAR DIARY
or
INTELLIGENCE SUMMARY
(Erase heading not required.)

Place	Date	Hour	Summary of Events and Information	Remarks and references to Appendices
RENINGHELST	16/12/15		1 Truck stores arrived including Bulk Soap, Rubbing Grease &c, 1080 Cape Mounted and 4 No 14 Periscopes	
RENINGHELST	17/12/15		1 Truck stores arrived including Horse Shoes, and 6000 Socks	
RENINGHELST	18/12/15		1 Truck stores arrived including Bulk S.O. Clothing and 985 ?	
RENINGHELST	19/12/15		2 Trucks stores arrived including bulk picketing gear and 1 Travelling Kitchen body for 5th London Regt	
RENINGHELST	20/12/15		3 Trucks including 1000 Blankets, Bulk Caps, Socks, Towels, Drawers, 1 G.S. Wagon for 23rd Battery, and 2 G.S. Wagons for 172 Tunnelling coy R.E. Sergt R and L/cpl ? Pte Davies A. Transferred to 5th corps for duty in office of A.D.O.S.	

Army Form C. 2118

WAR DIARY
or
INTELLIGENCE SUMMARY

(Erase heading not required.)

Instructions regarding War Diaries and Intelligence Summaries are contained in F. S. Regs., Part II. and the Staff Manual respectively. Title Pages will be prepared in manuscript.

Place	Date	Hour	Summary of Events and Information	Remarks and references to Appendices
Reninghelst	21/12/15		No stores today. 3000 Tube Helmets received from 5th Corps	
RENINGHELST	22/12/15		2 Trucks arrived including 14,495 Boots, 800 Drawers, 2 No 14 Reinsples and 1 Wagon light-plying for Cheshire F. Coy R.E., also Muzzle Protectors (Rifle) for Inf. Brigades.	
PENINGHELST	23/12/15		1 Truck stores arrived including Bulk Oil, Soap, Rations &c.	
PENINGHELST	24/12/15		N°. O. 6732 Pte J. Brown arrived from Calais for duty. 1 Truck arrived including Horse Shoes, 5 Bicycles, 254 Trench Helmets and 12 Lewis Guns	
PENINGHELST	25/12/15		1 Truck arrived including bulk S.D. Clothing and 1000 Satchels for Tube Helmets.	

Army Form C. 2118

WAR DIARY
or
INTELLIGENCE SUMMARY

(Erase heading not required.)

Instructions regarding War Diaries and Intelligence Summaries are contained in F. S. Regs., Part II. and the Staff Manual respectively. Title Pages will be prepared in manuscript.

Place	Date	Hour	Summary of Events and Information	Remarks and references to Appendices
RENINGHELST	26/12/15		1 Truck arrived including 1380 Macintosh Capes and Bulk general stores	
RENINGHELST	27/12/15		1 Truck arrived including Bulk Clothing and 3000 Goggles	
RENINGHELST	28/12/15		Truck arrived including 300 Brazier	
RENINGHELST	29/12/15		1 Truck arrived including 850 pr Boots, and 250 Lantern tent J.P.	
RENINGHELST	30/12/15		2 Trucks arrived including Bulk general stores, 100 Steel Trench Helmets ect. 1 G.S. Wagon for 2/R¹ Scots	

1875 Wt. W593/826 1,000,000 4/15 J.B.C. & A. A.D.S.S./Forms/C. 2118.

WAR DIARY
or
INTELLIGENCE SUMMARY

(Erase heading not required.)

Army Form C. 2118.

Place	Date	Hour	Summary of Events and Information	Remarks and references to Appendices
RENINGHELST	31/12/15		1 Truck containing Buck Horse Shoes, 2 Lamps Gen. Cart, Type and 20 Fire Extinguishers	

3RD DIVISION
DIVL. TROOPS

D.A.D.O.S.

JAN-DEC 1916.

3RD DIVISION
DIVL. TROOPS

Army Form C. 2118

WAR DIARY
or
INTELLIGENCE SUMMARY

(Erase heading not required.)

Instructions regarding War Diaries and Intelligence Summaries are contained in F. S. Regs., Part II. and the Staff Manual respectively. Title Pages will be prepared in manuscript.

Place	Date	Hour	Summary of Events and Information	Remarks and references to Appendices
RENINGHELST	1/6		2 Trucks arrived including Bulk Hose Shoes, Clothing & Personal Gear, 6000 Rations, 1000 Sloves Singulars, and 1 G.S. Limber Wagon for 2/R¹ Scots	
RENINGHELST	2/6		2 Trucks arrived including Bulk Picketing gear, 1 G.S. Wagon for 56 Coy R.E and 1 G.S. Wagon for 29th Battery, and 15 Lewis guns	
RENINGHELST	3/6		1 Truck arrived including Bulk Caps, Socks, Towels, and 1008 pr Gum Boots Thigh	
RENINGHELST	4/6		No stores arrived today	
RENINGHELST	5/6		2 Trucks arrived including 1 Limbered G.S. Wagon for 1/R¹ Scots Fus.	

Army Form C. 2118

WAR DIARY
or
INTELLIGENCE SUMMARY
(Erase heading not required.)

Instructions regarding War Diaries and Intelligence Summaries are contained in F. S. Regs., Part II. and the Staff Manual respectively. Title Pages will be prepared in manuscript.

Place	Date	Hour	Summary of Events and Information	Remarks and references to Appendices
RENINGHELST	6/10		1 Truck arrived including Bulk general stores	
RENINGHELST	7/10		2 Trucks arrived including Bulk Horse Shoes &c. Winter Drawers, Jerseys	
RENINGHELST	9/10		1 Truck arrived including Bulk Clothing	
RENINGHELST	10/10		3 Trucks arrived including Bulk Clothing and 1 G.S. Limbered Wagon for 1st R. Scots Fus. also 334 prs Trousers worn Boots, 400 Capes Waterstet, 200 Underpants pr. and 350 Leather Jerkins	
RENINGHELST	11/10		1 Truck arrived - Detail Issues, and 150 Capes Mackintosh	

1875 Wt. W593/826 1,000,000 4/15 J.B.C. & A. A.D.S.S./Forms/C. 2118.

Army Form C. 2118

WAR DIARY
or
INTELLIGENCE SUMMARY
(Erase heading not required.)

Instructions regarding War Diaries and Intelligence Summaries are contained in F. S. Regs., Part II. and the Staff Manual respectively. Title Pages will be prepared in manuscript.

Place	Date	Hour	Summary of Events and Information	Remarks and references to Appendices
RENINGHELST	12/11/15		1 Truck arrived including 950 Boots, 3000 femuris jugulum, 5000 2k and 6 Belts for M.G. for trial	D.O.O. 3rd DIVISION
RENINGHELST	13/11		1 Truck arrived including bulk general stores, 200 Open Musicled S. visited DDOS 2nd Army	D.O.O. 3rd DIVISION
RENINGHELST	14/11		2 Trucks arrived including bulk Horse Shoes, 4 W.W. Periscopes 1 G.S. Wagon for 150 Potters and 1 Hmi putsen G.S. Harness Wo 19 for gng East Yorks.	D.O.O. 3rd DIVISION
RENINGHELST	15/11		2 Trucks arrived including 1457 Magazines for Lewis gun, 500 Gm covers etc. 192 pr Short Irm Boots and Bush Clothing, also 1 G.S. Limbered Wagon 2/Royal Scots	D.O.O. 3rd DIVISION
RENINGHELST	16/11		1 Truck arrived including Horse Shoes, General Stores, &c.	D.O.O. 3rd DIVISION

1875 Wt. W593/826 1,000,000 4/15 J.B.C. & A. A.D.S.S./Forms/C. 2113.

Army Form C. 2118

WAR DIARY
or
INTELLIGENCE SUMMARY

(Erase heading not required.)

Instructions regarding War Diaries and Intelligence Summaries are contained in F.S. Regs., Part II. and the Staff Manual respectively. Title Pages will be prepared in manuscript.

Place	Date	Hour	Summary of Events and Information	Remarks and references to Appendices
RENINGHELST	17/10		1 Truck arrived including Bulk Clothing, 50 Wire Extractors, 35 Stewart's 50 French Patt. Helmets and 530 Horse Rugs	
RENINGHELST	18/10		2 Trucks arrived including 610 Jubilee bottles, 100 Capt. Macintosh, 500 Blankets 2 Sets Harness for M.G. Coy, and 1 G.S. Wagon for 3rd Siege Ary R.G.	
RENINGHELST	19/10		1 Truck arrived including 1145 Boots, 5 Zinc Baths etc.	
RENINGHELST	20/10		3 Trucks arrived including 5000 Shirts, bulk generalstores, 100 Utility Observers and 1 G.S. Limbered Wagon for 1/Gordon H. also 400 Trench Helmets	
RENINGHELST	21/10		1 Truck arrived including bulk Horse Shoes and detail stores	

1875 Wt. W593/826 1,000,000 4/15 J.B.C. & A. A.D.S.S./Forms/C. 2118.

Army Form C. 2118

WAR DIARY
or
INTELLIGENCE SUMMARY
(Erase heading not required.)

Instructions regarding War Diaries and Intelligence Summaries are contained in F.S. Regs., Part II. and the Staff Manual respectively. Title Pages will be prepared in manuscript.

Place	Date	Hour	Summary of Events and Information	Remarks and references to Appendices
RENINGHELST	22/16		1 Truck arrived including Boot Clothing Winter Khan, 4000 Hats woollen, 288 Special Small Helmets for R.A. and general stores	
RENINGHELST	23/16		1 Truck arrived including Boot General Stores, 10 Bugles, 30 Wheels, 330 Wagons for Lewis Guns, 108 pcs Iron Boots short, and 6 Boxes	
RENINGHELST	24/16		1 Truck stores including Clothing and general stores	
RENINGHELST	25/16		1 Truck arrived including 500 Drawers, 5000 Tube Helmets and ditto [?] also 350 Trench Helmets	
RENINGHELST	26/16		2 Trucks arrived including Gum Boots, Detail Stores, 1 G.S. Wagon for H.Q. Ox Train and 2 Hors Parks, G.S. Limbered Wagons for 4 Brotts Two	

1875 Wt. W503/826 1,000,000 4/15 J.B.C. & A. A.D.S.S./Forms/C.2118.

WAR DIARY
or
INTELLIGENCE SUMMARY

(Erase heading not required.)

Army Form C. 2118

Instructions regarding War Diaries and Intelligence Summaries are contained in F. S. Regs., Part II. and the Staff Manual respectively. Title Pages will be prepared in manuscript.

Place	Date	Hour	Summary of Events and Information	Remarks and references to Appendices
RENINGHELST	27th		3 Trucks arrived including half general stores, 500 P.H. Tube Helmets, 500 Mufflers and 1 Waistcoat for 2/Suffolks	
RENINGHELST	28th		2 Trucks arrived including tech Hors Shoes, 2900 P.H. Tube Helmets and detail stores, also 1 Lewis gun for 10th West Kens.	
RENINGHELST	29th		1 Truck arrived including Bulk Clothing, 300 Mufflers, detail stores and 1 Vickers gun	
RENINGHELST	30th		2 Trucks arrived including bulk General Stores, 12150 P.H. Helmets, 500 P.H. Hoods	
RENINGHELST	31st		1 Truck arrived including Bulk Clothing and detail stores	

Dunlop Lieut
1/West S. 3rd Div

Confidential

War Diary

of

DADOS. 3rd Division

From 1-2-16   to 29-2-16

Vol 19

Army Form C. 2118

WAR DIARY
or
INTELLIGENCE SUMMARY
(Erase heading not required.)

Instructions regarding War Diaries and Intelligence Summaries are contained in F. S. Regs., Part II. and the Staff Manual respectively. Title Pages will be prepared in manuscript.

Place	Date	Hour	Summary of Events and Information	Remarks and references to Appendices
RENINGHELST	1/2/16		1 Truck arrived including 400 Brown woollen, 150 French Helmets, 4 Steam-out Horse Clippers and detail stores. Also 52 Magazines Lewis gun for 10th W. Fus.	
RENINGHELST	2/2/16		3 Trucks arrived including 650 prs Boots, 4 Stewart Clipping Machines and detail stores also 9 West Bomb Throwers	
RENINGHELST	3/2/16		1 Truck arrived including Bush fences Stores &c, also 1 Store Pattern G.S. Limbered Wagon for 8th East Yorks	
RENINGHELST	4/2/16		2 Trucks arrived including Bulk Horseshoes, Detail Stores, 250 Frenchlets and 1 Hindpatten Limbered Wagon for 56. Coy R.E.	
RENINGHELST	5/2/16		No stores. Morning	

WAR DIARY
or
INTELLIGENCE SUMMARY

(Erase heading not required.)

Army Form C. 2118

Instructions regarding War Diaries and Intelligence Summaries are contained in F. S. Regs., Part II. and the Staff Manual respectively. Title Pages will be prepared in manuscript.

Place	Date	Hour	Summary of Events and Information	Remarks and references to Appendices
RENINGHELST	6/2/16		No stores Morning	
NORDAUSQUES	7/2/16		No stores. On Move	
NORDAUSQUES	8/2/16		No stores	
NORDAUSQUES	9/2/16		4 Lorry Loads stores drawn direct from Calais, including bulk clothing, General Stores, etc.	
NORDAUSQUES	10/2/16		4 Lorry Loads stores drawn direct from Calais, including bulk General Stores, Clothing, and Detail Stores	

1875 Wt. W503/826 1,000,000 4/15 J.B.C. & A. A.D.S.S./Forms/C. 2113.

WAR DIARY
or
INTELLIGENCE SUMMARY

Army Form C. 2118

Place	Date	Hour	Summary of Events and Information	Remarks and references to Appendices
NORDAUSQUES	11/7/16		4 Lorry Loads stores drawn direct from Calais including Bulk for Stores, Clothing and Detail Stores	
NORDAUSQUES	12/7/16		3 Lorry Loads stores drawn direct from Calais including Bulk General Stores and Detail Stores, also 1 Truck P.H. Helmets cleared from Railhead	
NORDAUSQUES	13/7/16		No stores today	
NORDAUSQUES	14/7/16		2 Trucks arrived including Bulk Clothing and General Stores, also 1 Maltese Cart for 13th King's Liverpool Regt	
NORDAUSQUES	15/7/16		3 Trucks arrived including General Stores, 1 G.S. Wagon for C.R.S., 1 Water Cart for 9th/10th N.F. Coy, 1 R.E. Limbered Wagon for Cheshire R.E., 1 Body R.E. Limber Wagon for East Riding R.E., 1 Body Travelling Kitchen for 12th West Yorks	

WAR DIARY
or
INTELLIGENCE SUMMARY

(Erase heading not required.)

Army Form C. 2118

Instructions regarding War Diaries and Intelligence Summaries are contained in F. S. Regs., Part II. and the Staff Manual respectively. Title Pages will be prepared in manuscript.

Place	Date	Hour	Summary of Events and Information	Remarks and references to Appendices
NORDAUSQUES	16/10		2 Trucks arrived including Bulk Boots, Detail Stores and 1 G.S. Wagon for S/o*JJJC*	
NORDAUSQUES	17/10		3 Trucks arrived including Bulk General Stores 15050 P.H. Helmets, 1 Travelling Kitchen and 1 Water Cart for 4th Royal Fusiliers and 1 Water Cart for Archie Fitter by R.S.	
NORDAUSQUES	18/10		3 Trucks arrived including Bulk Horse Shoes, Detail Stores, 3 Limbered Wagon Bodies for Sgt Ridway R.E., Waistcoat for 45th Battery, Officers Mess Cart for 3/P.S. Scots and 10th Welsh Fus., and 1 Fore Potion Limbered Wagon for 11th Battery, Stores for 96 Inf Bde sent by Lorry. S/Ser Holland L/Cpl Statham	
NORDAUSQUES	19/10		2 Trucks arrived including Bulk S.10. Clothing and 10 tail Stores	
NORDAUSQUES	20/10		2 Trucks arrived including Bulk General Stores, Detail Stores, and 1 Water Cart for 129th Battery	

1875 Wt. W593/826 1,000,000 4/15 J.B.C. & A. A.D.S.S./Forms/C. 2118.

WAR DIARY
or
INTELLIGENCE SUMMARY
(Erase heading not required.)

Army Form C. 2118

Instructions regarding War Diaries and Intelligence Summaries are contained in F. S. Regs., Part II. and the Staff Manual respectively. Title Pages will be prepared in manuscript.

Place	Date	Hour	Summary of Events and Information	Remarks and references to Appendices
NORDAUSQUES	21/2/16		6 Trucks arrived including Bulk Clothing, Detail Stores and S.G.S. Wagon for 3rd DAC	D.E.
NORDAUSQUES	22/2/16		2 Trucks arrived including Detail Stores and 1 Water Cart for 1st R. Scots F.	D.E.
NORDAUSQUES	23/2/16		No stores today	D.E.
NORDAUSQUES	24/2/16		3 Trucks arrived including Bulk Boots, General and Detail Stores. 1 G.S. Wagon for 8th East Yorks and 1 Water Cart for 23rd Bde R.F.A.	D.E.
NORDAUSQUES	25/2/16		1 Truck arrived including Bulk Horse Shoes and Detail Stores	D.E.

Army Form C. 2118

WAR DIARY
or
INTELLIGENCE SUMMARY
(Erase heading not required.)

Instructions regarding War Diaries and Intelligence Summaries are contained in F. S. Regs., Part II. and the Staff Manual respectively. Title Pages will be prepared in manuscript.

Place	Date	Hour	Summary of Events and Information	Remarks and references to Appendices
NORDAUSQUES	26/2/16		1 Truck arrived including Bulk Clothing and Detail Stores	
NORDAUSQUES	27/2/16		1 Truck arrived including Bulk General Stores &c.	
NORDAUSQUES	28/2/16		1 Truck arrived including Bulk Clothing and Detail Stores	
NORDAUSQUES	29/2/16		1 Truck arrived including Detail Stores, Cope Maintenance &c.	

Dunlop, Lieut
D.A.D.O.S. 3rd Divn

Confidential

War Diary

of

D.H.Q. V.S   3rd Division

From 1-3-16 to 31-3-16

Vol XX

Army Form C. 2118

WAR DIARY
or
INTELLIGENCE SUMMARY
(Erase heading not required.)

Instructions regarding War Diaries and Intelligence Summaries are contained in F.S. Regs., Part II. and the Staff Manual respectively. Title Pages will be prepared in manuscript.

Place	Date	Hour	Summary of Events and Information	Remarks and references to Appendices
NORDAUSQUES	1/7/16		1 Truck arrived including Boots, Sun goggles and detail stores. 9th Bde Staff went to join 17th Div.	
NORDAUSQUES	2/7/16		1 Truck arrived including Bath funeral Stores. Detail Stores and Sun goggles.	
NORDAUSQUES	3/7/16		1 Truck arrived including Bath Horse Shoes and detail stores. Also Pontoon boats for Cheshire Coy R.E.	
NORDAUSQUES	4/7/16		1 Truck arrived including Bath Clothing, detail stores and 2 Machine Guns for 9th Bde M.G. Coy	
NORDAUSQUES	5/7/16		2 Trucks arrived including Bath funeral Stores, Detail Stores and 1 R.S. Limbered Wagon for Sig Coy.	

Army Form C. 2118

WAR DIARY
or
INTELLIGENCE SUMMARY
(Erase heading not required.)

Instructions regarding War Diaries and Intelligence Summaries are contained in F. S. Regs., Part II. and the Staff Manual respectively. Title Pages will be prepared in manuscript.

Place	Date	Hour	Summary of Events and Information	Remarks and references to Appendices
NORDPEENE	6/12		No stores today. Heavy fall snow overnight. Trust Nails & Cops in demand	
NORDPEENE	7/12		No stores today	
NORDPEENE	8/12		Divn on move. No stores arrived	
RENINGHELST	9/12		More snow overnight. 1 truck arrived including Bulk General Stores Clothing, Boots, 15 Vermorel Sprayers etc	
RENINGHELST	10/12		4 Trucks arrived including Bulk Horse Shoes and 1 G.S. Wagon for 109th Battery	

1875 Wt. W⁹593/826 1,000,000 4/15 J.B.C. & A.   A.D.S.S./Forms/C. 2118.

Army Form C. 2118

WAR DIARY
or
INTELLIGENCE SUMMARY
(Erase heading not required.)

Instructions regarding War Diaries and Intelligence Summaries are contained in F. S. Regs., Part II. and the Staff Manual respectively. Title Pages will be prepared in manuscript.

Place	Date	Hour	Summary of Events and Information	Remarks and references to Appendices
RENINGHELST	11/3/16		3 Trucks arrived including Bulk Clothing, 100 Steel Helmets, 2000 prs from Boots thigh, detail stores, and 1 Lewis Gun for 10th W.Rid Fus Also 1 Wagon limber and 1 G.S.Wagon for 42nd Bde A.C. after repair	
RENINGHELST	12/3/16		1 Truck arrived including bulk general stores etc.	
RENINGHELST	13/3/16		3 Trucks arrived including Bulk Clothing, 420 prs F.S.Boots, and detail stores	
RENINGHELST	14/3/16		1 Truck arrived including Bulk Boots, 400 Steel Helmets, and detail stores, also 27 Radium Stoves	
RENINGHELST	15/3/16		1 Truck arrived including Detail stores &c	

1875 Wt. W593/826 1,000,000 4/15 J.B.C. & A. A.D.S.S./Forms/C. 2118.

Army Form C. 2118

WAR DIARY
or
INTELLIGENCE SUMMARY
(Erase heading not required.)

Instructions regarding War Diaries and Intelligence Summaries are contained in F.S. Regs., Part II. and the Staff Manual respectively. Title Pages will be prepared in manuscript.

Place	Date	Hour	Summary of Events and Information	Remarks and references to Appendices
RENINGHELST	16/3/16		1 Truck arrived today including Bulk general stores, detail stores, 5 Food Containers. Also 1 Vickers Gun for 3rd Motor M.G. By.	
RENINGHELST	17/3/16		4 Trucks arrived including 124 Boxes Horse Shoes, 1 Water Cart for 130th H. By, 1 Water Cart for 2nd Anglesey R.G., 1 Pontoon Wagon for East Riding R.E. and 1 G.S. Wagon for 42nd R.C.	
RENINGHELST	18/3/16		1 Truck arrived including Bulk Clothing, Detail Stores, and 400 Trench Helmets.	
RENINGHELST	19/3/16		1 Truck arrived including Bulk General Stores, Detail Stores etc.	
RENINGHELST	20/3/16		2 Trucks arrived including Bulk Clothing, Detail Stores and 1 Water Cart for 23rd Battery	

WAR DIARY
or
INTELLIGENCE SUMMARY
(Erase heading not required.)

Army Form C. 2118

Instructions regarding War Diaries and Intelligence Summaries are contained in F. S. Regs., Part II. and the Staff Manual respectively. Title Pages will be prepared in manuscript.

Place	Date	Hour	Summary of Events and Information	Remarks and references to Appendices
RENINGHELST	21/16		3 Trucks arrived including Retail Stores, 1 Limbered Wagon complete and 1 Hind [limber] Limbered Wagon for 9th Y.L. and 1 Wagon body Spring for East Riding R.G.	
RENINGHELST	22/16		1 Truck arrived including 1394 Boots, Retail Stores and slowing materials for Tents	
RENINGHELST	23/16		1 Truck arrived including Bulk general stores, Retail Stores, etc	
RENINGHELST	24/16		Heavy fall Snow overnight. 2 Trucks arrived including Bulk Horse Shoes, 2000 Steel Turret Helmets and Retail Stores	
RENINGHELST	25/16		3 Trucks arrived including Bulk Clothing, Sandbags, Retail Stores 1 Water cart for 129 Battery, and 1 S.S Wagon for 25 Bde R.F.A.	

1875 Wt. W593/826 1,000,000 4/15 J.B.C. & A. A.D.S.S./Forms/C. 2118.

Army Form C. 2118

WAR DIARY
or
INTELLIGENCE SUMMARY
(Erase heading not required.)

Instructions regarding War Diaries and Intelligence Summaries are contained in F. S. Regs., Part II. and the Staff Manual respectively. Title Pages will be prepared in manuscript.

Place	Date	Hour	Summary of Events and Information	Remarks and references to Appendices
RENINGHELST	26/3/16		2 Trucks arrived including Bulk general Stores, 10 bales Stores and 3y Lewis fun	
RENINGHELST	27/3/16		1 Truck arrived including Bulk Clothing, Detail Stores &c	
RENINGHELST	28/3/16		1 Truck arrived including Bulk Clothing, Cyles Macintosh and Detail Stores	
RENINGHELST	29/3/16		1 Truck arrived including 1580 prs Boots, Detail Stores, and 500 PH Helmets	
RENINGHELST	30/3/16		2 Trucks arrived including Bulk general stores, 1000 foggles, Detail Stores and 1 Lewis fun for 8th King's Own Lancs	

1875 Wt. W593/826 1,000,000 4/15 J.B.C. & A. A.D.S.S./Forms/C. 2118.

Army Form C. 2118

WAR DIARY
or
INTELLIGENCE SUMMARY
(Erase heading not required.)

Place	Date	Hour	Summary of Events and Information	Remarks and references to Appendices
RENINGHELST			1 Truck arrived including Bulk Horse Shoes, Detail Stores & 6 Horses Reinropes	

31/3/16

Shew Carl Capt.
DMS 3rd Div.

Vol XXI 3 12

Confidential
War Diary
of
D.A.D.O.S.   3rd Division

From 1-4-16 to 30-4-16

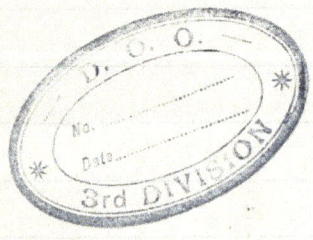

Army Form C. 2118

WAR DIARY
or
INTELLIGENCE SUMMARY
(Erase heading not required.)

Instructions regarding War Diaries and Intelligence Summaries are contained in F. S. Regs., Part II. and the Staff Manual respectively. Title Pages will be prepared in manuscript.

Place	Date	Hour	Summary of Events and Information	Remarks and references to Appendices
RENINGHELST	1/4/16		2 Trucks arrived including Boot Clothing, Detail Stores and 1 fore portion G.S. Limbered Wagon for 8th Leicesters	
RENINGHELST	2/4/16		1 Truck arrived including Boot General Stores, Detail Stores, etc	
FLETRE	3/4/16		Moved to Fletre. 1 Truck arrived including Boot Clothing, Detail Stores	
FLETRE	4/4/16		2 Trucks arrived including Boot Clothing, Detail Stores, 1 Vickers gun for 3rd M.M.L. Battery and 1 G.S. Wagon for 3 Section 3rd/1st F.C.	
FLETRE	5/4/16		1 Truck arrived including Boot Boots, Clothing and Detail Stores	

1875 Wt. W5o3/826 1,000,000 4/15 J.B.C. & A. A.D.S.S./Forms/C. 2113.

WAR DIARY or INTELLIGENCE SUMMARY

(Erase heading not required.)

Army Form C. 2118

Place	Date	Hour	Summary of Events and Information	Remarks and references to Appendices
FLETRE	6/4/16		1 Truck arrived including Bulk General Stores, Detail Stores and 388 Handles loading Magazine	
FLETRE	7/4/16		2 Trucks arrived including Bulk Horse Stores, Detail Stores and 1 G.S. Limbered Wagon for 172 Tunnelling Coy R.E. 1 Wagon limber for 2" Pottery and 1 Lewis Gun for 1/Gordon H.	
FLETRE	8/4/16		1 Truck arrived including Bulk Clothing, Detail Stores &c	
FLETRE	9/4/16		1 Truck arrived including Bulk General Stores, Detail Stores and 1 Vickers Gun for 8th Bde M.G. Coy	
FLETRE	10/4/16		2 Trucks arrived including Bulk Clothing, Detail Stores and Travelling Kitchen Body for 1/Gordon Highlanders	

Army Form C. 2118

WAR DIARY
or
INTELLIGENCE SUMMARY
(Erase heading not required.)

Place	Date	Hour	Summary of Events and Information	Remarks and references to Appendices
FLETRE	11/4/16		1 Truck arrived including Bulk Clothing, Detail Stores, 1 Maxim for 4th Royal Fus and 1 Mess Cart for 1/Gordons	
FLETRE	12/4/16		1 Truck arrived including Bulk Boots, Detail Stores, and 1 Lewis gun for 12th West Yorks	
FLETRE	13/4/16		1 Truck arrived including Bulk General Stores, Detail Stores &c.	
FLETRE	14/4/16		1 Truck arrived including Bulk Horse Shoes, Helmets and 1 Lewis gun for 1/R. Scots Fus. Lieut K.S. Morgan left for 3rd Army. 3rd/Div informed (59/16/59)	
FLETRE	15/4/16		1 Truck arrived including Bulk Clothing, Detail Stores and one 4.5" Howitzer for 130th Battery	

1875 Wt. W593/826 1,000,000 4/15 J.B.C. & A. A.D.S.S./Forms/C. 2118.

Army Form C. 2118

WAR DIARY
or
INTELLIGENCE SUMMARY

(Erase heading not required.)

Instructions regarding War Diaries and Intelligence Summaries are contained in F.S. Regs., Part II. and the Staff Manual respectively. Title Pages will be prepared in manuscript.

Place	Date	Hour	Summary of Events and Information	Remarks and references to Appendices
FLETRE	16/4/16		1 Truck arrived including Bulk General Stores, Clothing and Detail Stores	
FLETRE	17-4-16		1 Truck arrived including Bulk Clothing, Detail Stores &c.	
FLETRE	18-4-16		1 Truck arrived including General and Detail Stores	
FLETRE	19-4-16		1 Truck arrived including Bulk Boots and Detail Stores. 1 Enemy Machine gun and Carriage - captured by 'Nott' Fus at St Eloi sent to Base. Also 1 Vickers M. gun for Salvage.	
FLETRE	20-4-16		1 Truck arrived including Bulk General Stores, Detail Stores, &c. Also 1 Truck with 13870 P.H. Helmets - Div Reserve	

Army Form C. 2118

WAR DIARY
or
INTELLIGENCE SUMMARY
(Erase heading not required.)

Instructions regarding War Diaries and Intelligence Summaries are contained in F.S. Regs., Part II. and the Staff Manual respectively. Title Pages will be prepared in manuscript.

Place	Date	Hour	Summary of Events and Information	Remarks and references to Appendices
FLETRE	21/4/16		1 Truck arrived including Bulk Horse Shoes, Detail Stores and 4130 P.H Helmets to complete Div Reserve.	
FLETRE	22/4/16		1 Truck arrived including Bulk Clothing, Satellite and Supplies, Detail Stores etc.	
FLETRE	23/4/16		1 Truck arrived including Bulk General Stores, Detail Stores, etc.	
FLETRE	24/4/16		1 Truck arrived including Bulk Clothing, Detail Stores, etc	
FLETRE	25/4/16		No stores today	

WAR DIARY
or
INTELLIGENCE SUMMARY

Army Form C. 2118

Place	Date	Hour	Summary of Events and Information	Remarks and references to Appendices
FLETRE	26/4/16		2 Trucks arrived today including 1500 Box Respirators, Bulk Boots, Detail Stores and 1 G.S. Limbered Wagon for No.1 Coy Train. Moved to Westoutre	
WESTOUTRE	27/4/16		2 Trucks today including Bulk General Stores, Detail Stores and 1 W/S Cart for 2/ Suffolks. Pte Morris joined from Calais for duty	
WESTOUTRE	28/4/16		1 Truck arrived including Bulk Horse Shoes, 20 Tents, and Detail Stores Also 1 Limber for 7th Shop. L.F.	
WESTOUTRE	29/4/16		1 Truck arrived including Bulk Clothing, Detail Stores, Mineral Jelly, and 1090 Steel Trench Helmets	
WESTOUTRE	30/4/16		1 Truck arrived including Bulk Packeting Gear, General Stores, Solidets Goggles &c. Pte Hurley left for Calais.	Henry Earp Captain 19TH DSS Supt Div 30/4/16

Vol 22

Confidential
War Diary
of
D.A.D.O.S.   3rd Division

From 1-5-16 to 31-5-16

Army Form C. 2118

WAR DIARY
or
INTELLIGENCE SUMMARY
(Erase heading not required.)

Instructions regarding War Diaries and Intelligence Summaries are contained in F. S. Regs., Part II. and the Staff Manual respectively. Title Pages will be prepared in manuscript.

Place	Date	Hour	Summary of Events and Information	Remarks and references to Appendices
WESTOUTRE	1/5/16		2 Trucks arrived including Bulk Clothing, General Stores, Mineral Jelly, Trench Helmet covers, 1 Water Cart for 1/R.S.F. and 1 Travelling Kitchen for 1/R. Scots Fus.	
WESTOUTRE	2/5/16		2 Trucks arrived today including 2000 P.H. Helmets, Goggles, Satchel To Carry, Personnel Sprayers etc, and 1 R.E. limbered Wagon for 3rd Sig Coy R.E.	
WESTOUTRE	3/5/16		1 Truck arrived including Bulk Boots, 100 Steel Helmets, 494 Magazines for Lewis Guns, and Detail Stores	
WESTOUTRE	4/5/16		3 Trucks arrived including Bulk General Stores, 1000 Steel Helmets, 5 Telescopic Rifles, 1 Limber for 108 H. Battery and 1 Travelling Kitchen for 1/North'd Fus. D.A.D.O.S 2nd Army. inspection visit.	
WESTOUTRE	5/5/16		1 Truck arrived with Bulk Horse Shoes, Fringes Frontaux, 500 Smoke Helmets for Horses, Saddles, Goggles, and Detail Stores	

Army Form C. 2118

WAR DIARY
or
INTELLIGENCE SUMMARY
(Erase heading not required.)

Instructions regarding War Diaries and Intelligence Summaries are contained in F. S. Regs., Part II. and the Staff Manual respectively. Title Pages will be prepared in manuscript.

Place	Date	Hour	Summary of Events and Information	Remarks and references to Appendices
WESTOUTRE	6/5/16		2 Trucks arrived including Bulk Service Dress, Shirts, Drawers, and Detail Stores. Showery	
WESTOUTRE	7/5/16		1 Truck arrived including Bulk Several Stores, Goggles, P.H. Helmets and Detail Stores. Showery	
WESTOUTRE	8/5/16		1 Truck arrived including Bulk Clothing, 1000 P.H. Helmets, 1000 Towels, Helmet Covers, 4 Carriage Ambulance Stretchers and Detail Stores. Raining nearly all day.	
WESTOUTRE	9/5/16		1 Truck arrived including Detail Stores, Goggles and Solution. Raining all day	
WESTOUTRE	10/5/16		1 Truck arrived including Bulk Boots and Detail Stores, also P.H. Helmets and Goggles	

WAR DIARY
or
INTELLIGENCE SUMMARY

(Erase heading not required.)

Army Form C. 2118

Instructions regarding War Diaries and Intelligence Summaries are contained in F. S. Regs., Part II. and the Staff Manual respectively. Title Pages will be prepared in manuscript.

Place	Date	Hour	Summary of Events and Information	Remarks and references to Appendices
WESTOUTRE	11/5/16		1 Truck arrived including Bulk General Stores, Detail Stores &c.	[stamp: D.O.O. 3rd DIVISION]
WESTOUTRE	12/5/16		2 Trucks arrived including Bulk Horse Shoes and Detail Stores, also Water Cart for 2/Royal Scots. Showers.	[stamp: D.O.O. 3rd DIVISION]
WESTOUTRE	13/5/16		2 Trucks arrived including Bulk Clothing, P.H. Helmets, "Goggles", Detail Stores and 1 Travelling Kitchen Body for 4/Shrops. L.I. Rained all day.	[stamp: D.O.O. 3rd DIVISION]
WESTOUTRE	14/5/16		1 Truck arrived including Bulk General Stores, 20 Removal Sprays, 1000 Drawers for Laundry, and 6477 Coverings for Trench Helmets.	[stamp: D.O.O. 3rd DIVISION]
WESTOUTRE	15/5/16		1 Truck arrived including Bulk Clothing, and special consignment of Shirts, Socks & Drawers for Laundry	[stamp: D.O.O. 3rd DIVISION]

Army Form C. 2118

WAR DIARY
or
INTELLIGENCE SUMMARY
(Erase heading not required.)

Instructions regarding War Diaries and Intelligence Summaries are contained in F.S. Regs., Part II. and the Staff Manual respectively. Title Pages will be prepared in manuscript.

Place	Date	Hour	Summary of Events and Information	Remarks and references to Appendices
WESTOUTRE	16/5/16		2 Trucks arrived including Detail Stores, 2 Lewis Guns, 600 huyged Waistcoats and 7500 Satchels, also 1 Forage Cart for 8 & 9 Royal	
Westoutre	19/5/16		1 Truck arrived including Bulk Boots, Retail Stores, 36 Tents and 1000 P.H. Helmets. Also 1 Lewis Gun for 2 Royal Scots	
WESTOUTRE	18/5/16		2 Trucks arrived including Bulk Reserve Stores, Detail Stores, 1 G.S. Limbered Wagon for 2 Royal Scots and 1 Travelling Kitchen body for "Forden Helena"	
WESTOUTRE	19/5/16		1 Truck arrived including Bulk Horse Shoes, 15 Bicycles and detail stores	
WESTOUTRE	20/5/16		2 Trucks arrived including Bulk Clothing 10000 Satchels for Smoke Helmets, 4 3 inch Stokes Guns, Retail Stores and 3000 Steel Helmets	

Army Form C. 2118

WAR DIARY
or
INTELLIGENCE SUMMARY
(Erase heading not required.)

Instructions regarding War Diaries and Intelligence Summaries are contained in F.S. Regs., Part II. and the Staff Manual respectively. Title Pages will be prepared in manuscript.

Place	Date	Hour	Summary of Events and Information	Remarks and references to Appendices
WESTOUTRE	21/5/16		1 Truck arrived including Bulk picketing gear, 20 Tents and Detail Stores	
WESTOUTRE	22/5/16		1 Truck arrived including Bulk Clothing, 2000 PH Helmets, Detail Stores and 23 Lewis guns	
WESTOUTRE	23/5/16		1 Truck arrived including 450 Trousers, 6 Vermorel Sprayers, 10 Wet Stores, etc.	
WESTOUTRE	24/5/16		1 Truck arrived including 550 Boots, 25 Box Respirators and Detail Stores	
WESTOUTRE	25/5/16		2 Trucks arrived including Bulk General Stores, 600 Lewis Magazines, 1 Officers Mess Cart for 10 Battery, 1 Officers Mess Cart for 40 Wet H.Q., 1 Travelling Kitchen Body for 10 Wet Tren, Detail Stores, etc.	

WAR DIARY
or
INTELLIGENCE SUMMARY

(Erase heading not required.)

Army Form C. 2118

Place	Date	Hour	Summary of Events and Information	Remarks and references to Appendices
WESTOUTRE	26/5/16		2 Trucks arrived including Bulk Horse Shoes, 1000 Steel Helmet Covers, 1665 P.H.G. Helmets and Detail Stores	
WESTOUTRE	27/5/16		2 Trucks arrived including Bulk Clothing, 4 Stokes Guns, 1 S.A.A. Cart for No 1. Sect. D.A.C. and detail Stores. Moved to Flêtre	
FLÊTRE	28/5/16		1 Truck arrived including Bulk Second Stores, 1750 Steel Helmets, 1 Telescope Sight Rifle and Detail Stores	
FLÊTRE	29/5/16		1 Truck including Bulk Clothing, 542 Steel Helmets, 153 P.H.G. Helmets and Retail Stores	
FLÊTRE	30/5/16		1 Truck arrived including Retail Stores, 500 Lewis Magazines, and Sail Covers	

Army Form C. 2118

WAR DIARY
or
INTELLIGENCE SUMMARY

(Erase heading not required.)

Instructions regarding War Diaries and Intelligence Summaries are contained in F. S. Regs., Part II. and the Staff Manual respectively. Title Pages will be prepared in manuscript.

Place	Date	Hour	Summary of Events and Information	Remarks and references to Appendices
FLETRE	31/5/16		2 Trucks arrive including Bulk Boots, Retail Stores and 1 Travelling Kitchen for 13th West Yorks	

Owen Earp.
Captain.
1.97. A.9.S.3rd Div.

Confidential

War Diary

of

D.A.D.O.S. 3rd Division

From 1-6-16 to 30-6-16

Army Form C. 2118

WAR DIARY
or
INTELLIGENCE SUMMARY
(Erase heading not required.)

Instructions regarding War Diaries and Intelligence Summaries are contained in F.S. Regs., Part II. and the Staff Manual respectively. Title Pages will be prepared in manuscript.

Place	Date	Hour	Summary of Events and Information	Remarks and references to Appendices
FLETRE	1/6/16		1 Truck arrived including Bulk General Stores and Retail Stores	J.E.
FLETRE	2/6/16		1 Truck arrived including Bulk Horse Shoes and Retail Stores, also 1350 Satchels for Smoke Helmets	J.E.
FLETRE	3/6/16		1 Truck arrived including Bulk Clothing, Retail Stores and 8 Field Kitchens	J.E.
FLETRE	4/6/16		2 Trucks arrived including Bulk General Stores, Retail Stores, 434 Steel Helmets and 1 Water Cart for 7th King's Shrops L.I.	J.E.
FLETRE	5/6/16		2 Trucks including Bulk Clothing, 20 Hoss Carts for T.M. Batteries, 600 Waggoners for Transfunn and Retail Stores	J.E.

1875 Wt. W593/826 1,000,000 4/15 J.B.C. & A. A.D.S.S./Forms/C. 2118.

Army Form C. 2118

WAR DIARY
or
INTELLIGENCE SUMMARY
(Erase heading not required.)

Place	Date	Hour	Summary of Events and Information	Remarks and references to Appendices
FLETRE	6/10		1 Truck arrived including Retail Stores &c.	
FLETRE	7/10		1 Truck arrived including Bulk Boots, P.H.G. Helmets and Retail Stores	
FLETRE	8/10		2 Trucks arrived including Bulk General Stores and Retail Stores	
FLETRE	9/10		1 Truck arrived including Bulk Horse Shoes, Retail Stores and one 2nd Trench Howitzer for J.3. Battery	
FLETRE	10/10		2 Trucks arrived including Bulk Clothing, Retail Stores and 1 Hand portable G.S. Limbered Wagon for H.Q. Scots Fus.	

Army Form C. 2118

WAR DIARY
or
INTELLIGENCE SUMMARY
(Erase heading not required.)

Instructions regarding War Diaries and Intelligence Summaries are contained in F. S. Regs., Part II. and the Staff Manual respectively. Title Pages will be prepared in manuscript.

Place	Date	Hour	Summary of Events and Information	Remarks and references to Appendices
FLETRE	11/6		2 Trucks arrived including Bulk General Stores, Detail Stores and 1 G.S. Wagon for 129th Battery	
FLETRE	12/6		1 Truck arrived including Bulk Clothing, Detail Stores and 1000 Trench Helmet Covers	
FLETRE	13/6		2 Trucks arrived including 943 Trench Helmets, Detail Stores, 1 Water Cart for H.Q. 35th Div R.F.A. and 1 Water Cart for 6th Battery	
FLETRE	14/6		2 Trucks arrived including Bulk Boots, Detail Stores, and 1 Water Cart for 13th Liverpools	
FLETRE	15/6		1 Truck arrived including General Stores, Detail Stores &c.	

Army Form C. 2118

WAR DIARY
or
INTELLIGENCE SUMMARY

(Erase heading not required.)

Instructions regarding War Diaries and Intelligence Summaries are contained in F. S. Regs., Part II. and the Staff Manual respectively. Title Pages will be prepared in manuscript.

Place	Date	Hour	Summary of Events and Information	Remarks and references to Appendices
FLETRE	16/6/16		No stores today	
FLETRE	17/6/16		No stores today	
FLETRE	18/6/16		Moved to Tilques. No stores arrived	
TILQUES	19/6/16		1 Truck arrived including Bulk Clothing, Picketing Gear, Small Stores, 155 Special Lewis Magazines, 1000 Trench Helmet Covers, 202 N°9 Rifles and 300 Trench Helmets	
TILQUES	20/6/16		2 Trucks arrived including Bulk Clothing, Petrol Stores and 1 R.E. Limbered Wagon for Joplin Sig. Coy	

Army Form C. 2118

WAR DIARY
or
INTELLIGENCE SUMMARY

(Erase heading not required.)

Instructions regarding War Diaries and Intelligence Summaries are contained in F. S. Regs., Part II. and the Staff Manual respectively. Title Pages will be prepared in manuscript.

Place	Date	Hour	Summary of Events and Information	Remarks and references to Appendices
TILQUES	21/6/16		2 Trucks arrived including Bulk Boots, Retail Stores, 1 Water Cart for HQrs. L. Bomb., 1 Trav. Kitchen for 2/Suffolks, 1 Trav. Kitchen Body for 1/Gordons, etc.	
TILQUES	22/6/16		2 Trucks arrived including Bulk Horse Shoes, Forage Stores, Retail Stores, 2 Travelling Kitchens and 1 Body Telephone Wagon for HQ 76th Bde HQ.	
TILQUES	23/6/16		2 Trucks arrived including Bulk Horse Shoes, 6 Bicycles and 1 Retail Stores	
TILQUES	24/6/16		1 Truck arrived including Bulk Clothing, Retail Stores and 1 G.S. Wagon for 76th Bde M.G. Coy.	
TILQUES	25/6/16		2 Trucks arrived including Bulk Clothing, Picketing Gear, 1000 Steel Helmet Covers and 1 G.S. Limbered Wagon for 9th Bde M.G. Coy.	

Army Form C. 2118

WAR DIARY
or
INTELLIGENCE SUMMARY
(Erase heading not required.)

Instructions regarding War Diaries and Intelligence Summaries are contained in F.S. Regs., Part II. and the Staff Manual respectively. Title Pages will be prepared in manuscript.

Place	Date	Hour	Summary of Events and Information	Remarks and references to Appendices
TILQUES	26/6		1 Truck arrived including Bulk Clothing, 185 Lewis Magazines, Detail Stores &c	
TILQUES	27/6		1 Truck arrived including Bulk Clothing, Soap and Detail Stores	
TILQUES	28/6		1 Truck arrived today including Bulk Boots, Detail Stores &c	
TILQUES	29/6		3 Trucks arrived including Bulk General Stores. 1 Amm Wagon and 1 Limber for No 1. Sect. 1779a. 1 Travelling Kitchen body for 1 R. Scots and 1 pr Sergeant forks, also 1 Hindustan G.S. Limbered Wagon for 10th Welsh Fus.	
TILQUES	30/6		No Trucks today. Lorry sent to Calais to draw stores	

Rueufort Captain
OI/R.E. 3rd Division

Vol 24

Confidential

War Diary

of

D.A.D.O.S. 3rd Division

From 1-7-16 to 31-7-16

Army Form C. 2118.

WAR DIARY
or
INTELLIGENCE SUMMARY
(Erase heading not required.)

Instructions regarding War Diaries and Intelligence Summaries are contained in F. S. Regs., Part II. and the Staff Manual respectively. Title Pages will be prepared in manuscript.

Place	Date	Hour	Summary of Events and Information	Remarks and references to Appendices
TILQUES	1/7/16		Pr. Trucks arrived to-day. Division on move to 4th Army.	
TILQUES	2/7/16		No stores to-day. Moved from TILQUES to LE MEILLARD.	
LE MEILLARD	3/7/16		No stores to-day. On move to Vignacourt & Flesselles	
FLESSELLES	4/7/16		No stores to-day. On move to Cortée	
Cortée	5/7/16		No stores to-day	

Army Form C. 2118.

WAR DIARY
or
INTELLIGENCE SUMMARY
(Erase heading not required.)

Instructions regarding War Diaries and Intelligence Summaries are contained in F. S. Regs., Part II. and the Staff Manual respectively. Title Pages will be prepared in manuscript.

Place	Date	Hour	Summary of Events and Information	Remarks and references to Appendices
CORBIE	6/7/16		No stores today. 189th/Scottish Horse visited Dump. 49 Handcarts for Trench Mortars received from 4th Tyneng Workshops and distributed to Bdes.	R.E.
CORBIE	7/7/16		No stores today	R.E.
CORBIE	8/7/16		No stores today. Moved to Bray Sur Somme	R.E.
BRAY SUR SOMME	9/7/16		1 Truck arrived containing Bulk Blotting, Pickling Scansliver at Stores Suggles and Detail Stores	R.E.
BRAY SUR SOMME	10/7/16		4 Trucks arrived including Bulk Clothing, Boots, General and Detail Stores Goggles, 637 Box Respirators, 1000 Satchels &c, and 73 Lewisgun Hand Carts	R.E.

Army Form C. 2118.

WAR DIARY
or
INTELLIGENCE SUMMARY

(Erase heading not required.)

Instructions regarding War Diaries and Intelligence Summaries are contained in F. S. Regs., Part II. and the Staff Manual respectively. Title Pages will be prepared in manuscript.

Place	Date	Hour	Summary of Events and Information	Remarks and references to Appendices
BRAY SUR SOMME	2/11/16		3 Trucks arrived including 71 Lewisjohn Hand Carts. Informed by Havre that no Bulk Demands have been transferred from Calais. Notification received from Calais that Bulk Demands were being cancelled. Mud encumbrances caused units in particular Army Lines, in need of Horse Shoes, Boots, Oil, Grease, etc. Remounts submitted to Havre.	
BRAY SUR SOMME	12/7/16		1 Truck arrived including 532 Boots, 462 Magazines for Lewis Guns, no Rail Cars. Still no Horse Shoes, Oil &c. Mineral Oil urgently needed for guns, supply borrowed from 9th Division Somme. Detail Stores &c.	
BRAY SUR SOMME	13/7/16		2 Trucks arrived containing Sketches and Blankets for A.D.M.S. Still no Horse Shoes, Oil &c. Mirror Camp.	
BRAY SUR SOMME	14/7/16		1 Truck arrived including Bulk Oil, Soap, Grease, Horse Shoes, Detail Stores &c. Parity Horse Shoes sent by Havre instead of Boxes as demanded. Mirror Camp.	
BRAY SUR SOMME	15/7/16		2 Trucks arrived including Bulk Oil, Soap, Grease, Horse Shoes, Clothing, 465 Lewis's Magazines, Detail Stores &c. 3 Trucks Vehicles arrived including 1 Pontoon Wagon and 1 Limbered Wagon for Stokes Trench Cap R.E. Transp Kitchen Bodys for 2/Resets. 1 Fire Limber for 17th F. and 1 Water Cart each for 29 Battery, 2/Suffolks and 12th West Yorks	

Army Form C. 2118.

WAR DIARY
or
INTELLIGENCE SUMMARY
(Erase heading not required.)

Instructions regarding War Diaries and Intelligence Summaries are contained in F. S. Regs., Part II. and the Staff Manual respectively. Title Pages will be prepared in manuscript.

Place	Date	Hour	Summary of Events and Information	Remarks and references to Appendices
BRAY SUR SOMME	16/7/16		Issued. No stores arrived today although 2 Trucks advised and due today. 2 Trucks arrived with 1 Lantern Wagon, 8 Riding Pads, 1 Travelling Kitchen for 8th East Yorks and 1 Water Cart for 5th Pk Scots. No May Dills with vehicles. 3 Lewis Guns demanded by 7th Shrops. Lt. H. to replace other Lt. Guns in wagons.	
BRAY SUR SOMME	17/7/16		H.D.O.S. visited Brugh and recommended move to GROVETOWN. 4 Trucks arrived including Bulk Clothing, Picketing Gear, 281 Boxes Horse Shoes, General and Detail Stores etc &c. 3 Lewis Guns received for 12th Shrops. 2 Vickers Guns demanded by 9th Bde M.G. Coy to replace others disposed of in action.	
BRAY SUR SOMME	18/7/16		1 Truck arrived including Detail Stores and 72 gallons Buffer Oil. 1 Vickers Gun demanded for 8th Bde M.G. Coy. 2 Lewis Guns demanded for 1st R. Scots Fus.	
BRAY SUR SOMME	19/7/16		1 Truck advised but has not arrived. 2 Lewis Guns obtained from O.C. Army Troops for 13th Liverpools and 1 for 12th W. Yorks.	
BRAY SUR SOMME	20/7/16		1 Truck arrived including Bulk Oil, Soap, Dubbin, Detail Stores &c. 10 Captured M.G. handed over to R.O.O. for despatch to Base. May Bill dated 19/7/16. 13th Liverpools 3, 12th West Yorks 2, 2nd Royal Scots 3, 8th East Yorks 1, 1st Glos Scots Fus. 1, R.E. Signal Coy and Divnl Engineers Ranger finder 13th Liverpool. 2 Lewis Guns demanded for 8th East Yorks.	

Forms/C.2118/12.

Army Form C. 2118.

WAR DIARY
or
INTELLIGENCE SUMMARY
(Erase heading not required.)

Instructions regarding War Diaries and Intelligence Summaries are contained in F. S. Regs., Part II. and the Staff Manual respectively. Title Pages will be prepared in manuscript.

Place	Date	Hour	Summary of Events and Information	Remarks and references to Appendices
BRAY sur SOMME	21/7/16		2 Trucks arrived including Bulk Horse Shoes, 500 Trench Helmets, Detail Stores, 1 Fore Limber for 2/Suffolks and 1 Travelling Kitchen Body for 2nd R.Scots and 18pr. Gun Carriage components for 4.5" Battery to replace gun destroyed by the 8th K.R. Rifles. 1 Lewis Gun armourer for 8th K.R. Rifles. Steel Stores.	
BRAY sur SOMME	22/7/16		3 Trucks arrived today including Bulk Artillery, Horse Shoes, Gun Supplies, Helmets viz. 1292 prs Boots, 1000 Steel Helmets, Detail Stores and 1 Mem Cart for 7th Shrops L.I. 1 Vickers Gun for 8th Norf M.G. Coy and 2 Lewis Guns "R.S gts." received from Abbeville. 1 Captured M.G. (Maxim Pattern) and 1 Captured automatic rifle sent to Base. 3 Lewis Guns armourer for 10th Welch Fus.	
BRAY sur SOMME	23/7/16		3 Lewis Gun armourers, 2 for 8th East Yorks and 1 for 8th K.O.Yorks L.I. No Trucks arrived from Base. One 18pr. Gun & carriage arrived at MERICOURT for 4.5" Battery.	
BRAY sur Som	24/7/16		1 Truck arrived including bulk Shells, Socks, Towels &c, Picketing gear, Camp Equip., Necessaries and Detail Stores. 3 Lewis Guns arrived from Abbeville for 10th Welch Fus.	
BRAY sur SOMME	25/7/16		No Trucks arrived today. 1 Lewis gun armourer for 8th East Yorks.	

Army Form C. 2118.

WAR DIARY
or
INTELLIGENCE SUMMARY
(Erase heading not required.)

Instructions regarding War Diaries and Intelligence Summaries are contained in F.S. Regs., Part II. and the Staff Manual respectively. Title Pages will be prepared in manuscript.

Place	Date	Hour	Summary of Events and Information	Remarks and references to Appendices
BRAY SUR SOMME	26/7/16		2 Trucks arrived including Butt Boots (12 prs) 535prs Pantaloons, 300 Lewis Magazines, 40 Very Pistols, 800 Shirts, 900 Socks, Butt Badges and Ammun., Detail Stores &c. 1 Motor Car for 4/R.F., 2 Waterproof Sheets for 1/Gordons, 1 Trav. Kitchen Cooker for 12th West Yorks. 1 Lewis Gun arrived for 8/8 Yorks and 1 18pr. for 29th Battery	
BRAY SUR SOMME	27/7/16		Moved to TREUX. 1 Truck arrived including Butt Oil, Soap, Dubbing &c. Accoutrements Saivers & Shoemakers materials &c. 2 Lewis Guns demanded to replace Lewis &c.	
TREUX	28/7/16		1 Truck arrived including Butt Horse Shoes and 1000 Steel Helmets also Detail Stores. 2 Vickers Guns demanded for 9th M.G. Coy and 1 Lewis Gun for 8/8 Yorks. 2.18pr Guns demanded. 1 each for 6th and 49th Batteries.	
TREUX	29/7/16		2 Trucks arrived including Butt Underclothing, Service 10cwn, Detail Stores, 1 Limbered Wagon for 56 Coy R.E. and 1 G.S. Wagon for No. 1 Section D.A.C. 8 Lewis Guns arrived 3 for 1/D.S.F. 3 for 4/R.F. 1 for 8/Suffolks and 1 for 9/Sheffield L.I.	
TREUX	30/7/16		1 Truck arrived including Butt Picketing Gear, General Stores, Detail Stores &c. Also Truck with 2 18pr Guns, 1 each for 6th and 49th Batteries. 3 Lewis Guns demanded for 1/London Scot.	

Army Form C. 2118.

WAR DIARY
or
INTELLIGENCE SUMMARY

(Erase heading not required.)

Place	Date	Hour	Summary of Events and Information	Remarks and references to Appendices
TREUX	31/7/16		1. Truck arrived containing 1 18pr Gun for 108th Battery R.F.A. 2. Vickers guns each for 8th and 9th M.G. Coys and 1 Lewis Gun for 3rd East Yorks	

P. Newkirk.
Captain.

Vol 25

Confidential

War Diary

of

D.A.D.O.S. 3rd Division

From 1-8-16 to 31-8-16

Army Form C. 2118.

WAR DIARY
or
INTELLIGENCE SUMMARY

(Erase heading not required.)

Instructions regarding War Diaries and Intelligence Summaries are contained in F. S. Regs., Part II. and the Staff Manual respectively. Title Pages will be prepared in manuscript.

Place	Date	Hour	Summary of Events and Information	Remarks and references to Appendices
TREUX (Somme)	1/8/16		3 Trucks arrived including Bulk Clothing, Necessaries, finding and Shoemakers Materials, 1 Limbered Wagon for 56 Coy R.E, 1 Mess Cart for 129th Battery, 2 Q.F. 18 Pounders – 1 each for 23rd & 49th Bys, 1 Stokes Gun for 76/1. T.M. By, 1 Vickers Gun for 9th M.G. Coy, 6 Lewis Guns – 3 each for 1st Rs Scots and 7/R.S. Scots	
TREUX (Somme)	2/8/16		2 Trucks arrived including Bulk Clothing, Boots, Gas Helmets &c, Aubrey Oil Lamps &c, 160 Revolvers, 1 Water Cart for 107th Battery, 1 Mess Cart for 7 Suffolks, 1 Hand Limber for 76th M.G. Coy, 1 complete limbered Wagon for 8th Bn M.G. Coy. 1 Vickers gun demanded for 8th M.G. Coy	
TREUX (Somme)	3/8/16		No Trucks arrived	
TREUX (Somme)	4/8/16		2 Trucks arrived including Bulk General Stores, Running Cart Stores, 10 2" Rifles for Lewis Guns, and 800 Steel Helmets. Also 1 Water Cart for 7/R.S. Scots	
TREUX (Somme)	5/8/16		2 Trucks arrived including Bulk Clothing, General Stores and 1 Vickers Gun for 8th M.G. Coy	

Army Form C. 2118.

WAR DIARY
or
INTELLIGENCE SUMMARY

(Erase heading not required.)

Instructions regarding War Diaries and Intelligence Summaries are contained in F. S. Regs., Part II. and the Staff Manual respectively. Title Pages will be prepared in manuscript.

Place	Date	Hour	Summary of Events and Information	Remarks and references to Appendices
TREUX (SOMME)	6/8/16		1 Truck arrived including 5 Vickers Guns for 9th M.G. Coy and Running Out Springs for 4.5" Howitzers. 3. 1 Str Jury and 1-4.5" Howitzer arrived at Pekeus. Handed over to Coy Workshop Coffin	D.A.D.O.S. 3rd DIVISION
TREUX (SOMME)	7/8/16		3 Trucks arrived including Bulk Supplied Stores, Clothing and Retail Stores, also 16 Vehicle wheels, 1 Limbered Wagn. cord for 9th M.G. Coy and 4 type Fan., 1 Travelling Kitchen Body — and 1 Water Cart for 20th R.R.	D.A.D.O.S. 3rd DIVISION
TREUX (SOMME)	8/8/16		1 Truck arrived including bulk Clothing, Necessaries, Shoemakers and Saddlery Stores, Lewis Magazines, etc.	D.A.D.O.S. 3rd DIVISION
TREUX (SOMME)	9/8/16		1 Truck arrived including Bulk Boots, Sun Helmets &c, Satchels	D.A.D.O.S. 3rd DIVISION
TREUX (SOMME)	10/8/16		1 Truck arrived including bulk Accoutrements, Rasing, Oils, Soap, &c, Retail Stores and 1532 Magazines for Lewis Guns.	D.A.D.O.S. 3rd DIVISION

Army Form C. 2118.

WAR DIARY
or
INTELLIGENCE SUMMARY

(Erase heading not required.)

Instructions regarding War Diaries and Intelligence Summaries are contained in F. S. Regs., Part II. and the Staff Manual respectively. Title Pages will be prepared in manuscript.

Place	Date	Hour	Summary of Events and Information	Remarks and references to Appendices
TREUX (SOMME)	11/8/16		1 Truck arrived including Bath Horse Shoes, Smoke Helmets &c	D.A.D.O.S. 3rd DIVISION
TREUX (SOMME)	12/8/16		1 Truck arrived including Bath General Stores, Clothing, Magazines for Lewis Guns, etc &c. Moved to Grove Town	D.A.D.O.S. 3rd DIVISION
GROVETOWN (SOMME)	13/8/16		2 Trucks arrived including Bath General Stores, Packing Gear &c, also 2 Water Carts, 1 each for 29th F.K.R.R. and 49th Battery. Moved to Forked Tree	D.A.D.O.S. DIVISION
FORKED TREE (SOMME)	14/8/16		1 Truck general stores. 600 Steel Helmets received from 13th Corps, also 5 Hand Carts	D.A.D.O.S. 3rd DIVISION
FORKED TREE (SOMME)	15/8/16		1 Truck arrived including Bath General Stores, Clothing and detail stores 900 Steel Helmets from 55th Division	D.A.D.O.S. DIVISION

Army Form C. 2118.

WAR DIARY
or
INTELLIGENCE SUMMARY
(Erase heading not required.)

Instructions regarding War Diaries and Intelligence Summaries are contained in F. S. Regs., Part II. and the Staff Manual respectively. Title Pages will be prepared in manuscript.

Place	Date	Hour	Summary of Events and Information	Remarks and references to Appendices
FORKEDTREE (SOMME)	16/8/16		No Trucks today. 1 Heavy T. McGlew received from Corps and sent to TMC	D.A.D.O.S. [initials]
FORKEDTREE (SOMME)	17/8/16		Transferred to XIV Corps from Midnight. 1 Truck today including Bulk Boots, Oils, Soft, General Stores, Clothing, P.H.G. Helmets. Accoutrements and 500 Steel Helmets	D.A.D.O.S. 30th DIV. [initials]
FORKEDTREES (SOMME)	18/8/16		1 Truck today including Bulk Horse Shoes, Detail Stores, 1000 Steel Helmets, 1000 P.H. Helmets etc. 2 Vickers guns demanded for 9 M.G. Coy	D.A.D.O.S. [initials]
FORKEDTREE (SOMME)	19/8/16		1 Truck arrived including Bulk Clothing, Oil, P.H.G. Helmets and Detail Stores	D.A.D.O.S. 3rd DIVISION [initials]
FORKEDTREE (SOMME)	20/8/16		1 Truck arrived including Bulk General Stores, Picketing Gear, P.H.G. Helmets, Running Out Springs etc, 1 Hood and 3 Fore Limbers for 10th West Yorks. 2 Lewis Guns demanded for [crossed out] 12th West Yorks	D.A.D.O.S. 3rd DIVISION [initials]

Army Form C. 2118.

WAR DIARY
or
INTELLIGENCE SUMMARY

(Erase heading not required.)

Instructions regarding War Diaries and Intelligence Summaries are contained in F. S. Regs., Part II. and the Staff Manual respectively. Title Pages will be prepared in manuscript.

Place	Date	Hour	Summary of Events and Information	Remarks and references to Appendices
FORKED TREE (SOMME)	21/7/16		1 Tank stores arrived including Both Clothing, Necessaries, Satchels, Jumping and P.H.G. Helmets. Compasses and Pte Seels attached to Amiens 35th Divn. for Artillery reconn.	D.A.D.O.S. 3rd Divn.
FORKETREE (SOMME)	22/7/16		No stores arrived. 1. Lewis Gun arrived for 12/W.Yorks.	D.A.D.O.S. 3rd Divisn.
TREUX (SOMME)	23/7/16		No stores arrived. Moved to BERNAVILLE	D.A.D.O.S. 3rd Divisn.
BERNAVILLE (SOMME)	24/8/16		No stores today. Truck arrived at Borque Maison next journey to Rottens	D.A.D.O.S. 3rd Divisn.
BERNAVILLE (SOMME)	25/7/16		No stores today. Moved to Fienvillers-Grand (Somme)	D.A.D.O.S.

Army Form C. 2118.

WAR DIARY
or
INTELLIGENCE SUMMARY
(Erase heading not required.)

Instructions regarding War Diaries and Intelligence Summaries are contained in F. S. Regs., Part II. and the Staff Manual respectively. Title Pages will be prepared in manuscript.

Place	Date	Hour	Summary of Events and Information	Remarks and references to Appendices
Fricken le Grand (Somme)	9/6/16		No stores today. Moved to Flers	D.A.D.O.S., 3rd DIVISION. JE.
Flers	27/6/16		No stores today. Moved to NOEUX les MINES - 1st Corps First Army	D.A.D.O.S., 3rd DIVISION. JE.
NOEUX les MINES	28/8/16		Truck arrived with stores loaded at GROVETOWN. Third from 17905 1st Corps	D.A.D.O.S., 3rd DIVISION. JE.
NOEUX les MINES	29/8/16		1 Truck arrived with 3 fne and 1 Hind Jenkers for 10th Welch Fus.	D.A.D.O.S., 3rd DIVISION. JE.
NOEUX les MINES	30/8/16		1 Truck arrived with General Stores. No vouchers or Way Bills	D.A.D.O.S., 3rd DIVISION. JE.

Army Form C. 2118.

WAR DIARY
or
INTELLIGENCE SUMMARY
(Erase heading not required.)

Place	Date	Hour	Summary of Events and Information	Remarks and references to Appendices
NOEUX les Mines	31/8/16		2 Trucks arrived including 850 Boots, 2000 Shirts, 4,700 Socks, etc. General Stores and 9 Lewis Guns	[stamp: D.A.D.O.S. 3rd DIVISION] Stewartsp. Captain. [stamp: D.A.D.O.S. 3rd DIVISION. Date 31/8/16]

Vol 26

Confidential War Diary

DADOS 3rd Div

1-9-16 to 30-9-16

Army Form C. 2118.

WAR DIARY
or
INTELLIGENCE SUMMARY

(Erase heading not required.)

Instructions regarding War Diaries and Intelligence Summaries are contained in F. S. Regs., Part II. and the Staff Manual respectively. Title Pages will be prepared in manuscript.

Place	Date	Hour	Summary of Events and Information	Remarks and references to Appendices
NOEUX les Mines	1 9/16		3 Trucks arrived including Bulk Clothing, General Stores Accoutrements etc. 1500 P.H.G. Smoke Helmets Also 1 Travelling Kitchen for 8th Kings Gun Laws and 1 Fire Loader for 1st Royal Scots Fus.	D.A.D.O.S 3rd DIVISION [initials]
NOEUX les Mines	2 9/16		1 Truck arrived including Bulk General Stores, Detail Stores, 1900 P.H.G. Helmets and 2 Lewis Guns for 7 Yorkshire L.I.	D.A.D.O.S. 3rd DIVISION [initials]
NOEUX les Mines	3 9/16		1 Truck arrived including Bulk Clothing, General Stores, Detail Stores etc. and 2 Lewis Guns for 1st Gordons. Visited D.D.O.S. 1st Army. Instructed to complete Pioneer Batt. (20th KRR) to full complement of Lewis Guns	D.A.D.O.S 3rd DIVISION [initials]
NOEUX les Mines	4 9/16		1 Truck arrived including Bulk Perketing Soap, General Stores, 500 Lewis Magazines and 1500 Satchels antigas	D.A.D.O.S. DIVISION [initials]
NOEUX les Mines	5 9/16		2 Trucks arrived including Bulk Clothing, Detail Stores and 1 Water Cart for 8 Field Ambulance	D.D.O.S. DIVISION [initials]

Army Form C. 2118.

WAR DIARY
or
INTELLIGENCE SUMMARY
(Erase heading not required.)

Instructions regarding War Diaries and Intelligence Summaries are contained in F. S. Regs., Part II. and the Staff Manual respectively. Title Pages will be prepared in manuscript.

Place	Date	Hour	Summary of Events and Information	Remarks and references to Appendices
NOEUX les Mines	6/9/16		2 Trucks arrived including General Stores, 1500 Shels, 1250 Lewis Magazines, 33 Bicycles, 3000 P.H.G. Helmets and detail stores. Demand for P.H.G. Helmets complete	D.A.D.O.S. 3rd DIVISION
NEUX les Mines	7/9/16		2 Trucks arrived including Boots and Clothing, Detail Stores also 1 Water Cart for 9th F. Amb and 1 Heir Limber for 10th Md Fd	D.A.D.O.S. 3rd DIVISION
NOEUX les Mines	8/9/16		2 Trucks arrived including Boots General Stores, Accoutrements, General Stores and Detail Stores, also 1 Water Cart for 8th Kings Own Lewis	D.A.D.O.S. 3rd DIVISION
NEUX les Mines	9/9/16		3 Trucks arrived including Bulk Horse Shoes, Saddles antigas, 1548 Lewis Boots, 1 Water Cart for 1/N.7 and 1 cooper's G.S. Limbered Wagon for 8th M.G. Coy	D.A.D.O.S. 3rd DIVISION
NEUX les Mines	10/9/16		4 Trucks arrived including Bulk Clothing, General Stores, 6 Lewis Guns for 20th R.R., 1248 Lewis Boots Thigh, 3160 Blankets &c	D.A.D.O.S. 3rd DIVISION

WAR DIARY or INTELLIGENCE SUMMARY

Army Form C. 2118.

Place	Date	Hour	Summary of Events and Information	Remarks and references to Appendices
NOEUX les Mines	11/9/16		2 Trucks arrived including Bulk General Stores, 1700 Trousers Puttees, Clothing Badges etc, and 1212 prs Lanc Boots High. 1 4.5 How and Carriage also received by 10.93 Battery	
NOEUX les Mines	13/9/16		1 Truck arrived including 2000 Shirts, 1000 Drawers, 64 Periscopes No 9, 1189 Steel Helmet Covers, 1600 Rifle Breech Covers, 8000 Soles & Heels for Lanc Boots, Tools for Armourers Staff and Detail Stores	
NOEUX les Mines	14/9/16		3 Trucks arrived including Bulk Boots, General Stores, 3000 Blankets and 1 complete G.S. Limbered Wagon each for 1/N.F. and 4th R.F.	
NOEUX les Mines	15/9/16		2 Trucks arrived including General Stores, Accoutrements, 1700 Blankets, Detail Stores and 1 Lewis Gun for 4th Rif Brig	D.A.D.O.S. 3rd DIVISION
NOEUX les Mines	16/9/16		4 Trucks arrived including General Stores, Horse Shoes, 95 vehicle Wheels, 2050 Blankets, 1 Travelling Kitchen for 13 Lanfords, 1 18 Pr for 6th Battery and 1 Carriage 18 Pr each for 6th and 45th Batteries	

WAR DIARY
or
INTELLIGENCE SUMMARY

(Erase heading not required.)

Army Form C. 2118.

Place	Date	Hour	Summary of Events and Information	Remarks and references to Appendices
NŒUX les Mines	17/9/16		3 Trucks arrived including Bulk Clothing, General Stores, 24 Medl. Wagon Equipt. 3150 Blankets and 750 F.S. Boots.	D.A.D.O.S. 3rd DIVISION
NŒUX les Mines	18/9/16		1 Truck arrived including General Stores, Picketing Gear, 28 Medl. 1500 Steel Helmets sent in own distribution 500 to 8th Divn., 1000 to 9th Corps.	D.A.D.O.S. 3rd DIVISION
NŒUX les Mines	19/9/16		1 Truck arrived including Bulk Necessaries, Saddlery, General Stores etc.	D.A.D.O.S. 3rd DIVISION
NŒUX les Mines	20/9/16		3 Trucks arrived including General Stores, 35 Sayers Stoves, 50 Wagon Wheels, detail stores and 1 Water cart and for 45 Hy. By. and 20th K.R.R.	D.A.D.O.S. 3rd DIVISION
NŒUX les Mines	21/9/16		1 Truck arrived including Bulk Boots, 40 C.S.L. Tents, 3 Operating Tents etc etc.	D.A.D.O.S. 3rd DIVISION

Army Form C. 2118.

WAR DIARY
or
INTELLIGENCE SUMMARY
(Erase heading not required.)

Instructions regarding War Diaries and Intelligence Summaries are contained in F. S. Regs., Part II. and the Staff Manual respectively. Title Pages will be prepared in manuscript.

Place	Date	Hour	Summary of Events and Information	Remarks and references to Appendices
Nieux les Mines	22/6		No Stores except 1 Water Cart for 9th Field Amb. Move to BOMY	D.A.D.O.S. 3rd DIVISION
BOMY	23/6		No Stores arrived from Base. Balance of Stores brought from NIEUX LES MINES	A.D.O.S. 3rd DIVISION
BOMY	24/6		No stores arrived. Purchased Materials at Hazebrouck & Aire	D.O.S. G.H.Q.
BOMY	25/6		No Stores arrived. Lorry sent to NOEUX les MINES for Clothing &c. Purchased Materials at Hazebrouck.	D.A.D.O.S. 3rd DIVISION
BOMY	26/6		15 Ton General Stores arrived including 500 F.S. Books, Horse Shoes, Clothing, Helmet Covers, Cable for Signals, Picketing Gear etc. also 1 Limber for 4th Royal Fus. and 1 Fore limber for Lewis pistols for 3rd.	D.A.O.S. 3rd DIVISION

2449 Wt. W14957/M90 750,000 1/16 J.B.C. & A. Forms/C.2118/12.

Army Form C. 2118.

WAR DIARY
or
INTELLIGENCE SUMMARY
(Erase heading not required.)

Instructions regarding War Diaries and Intelligence Summaries are contained in F. S. Regs., Part II. and the Staff Manual respectively. Title Pages will be prepared in manuscript.

Place	Date	Hour	Summary of Events and Information	Remarks and references to Appendices
BONY	27/9/16		2 Trucks arrived including 8 Tons General Stores, Acc's, Picketing Gear, Oil Paint &c., and 4 Tons Clothing, Socks, Towels &c. D.A.D.O.S. Field Fumigator Dump.	D.A.D.O.S. 3rd DIVISION
BONY	28/9/16		1 Truck arrived including Boots, Soxlets, Running Acc Springs Oval Stoves, etc.	D.A.D.O.S. 3rd DIVISION
BONY	29/9/16		1 Truck arrived including Bulk General Stores, Soxlets, Acc's, Primus Cartridges, etc	D.A.D.O.S. 3rd DIVISION
BONY	30/9/16		1 Truck arrived including Bulk Horse Shoes, General and Oval Stoves	D.A.D.O.S. 3rd DIVISION

Percy Carp
Captain
D.A.D.O.S.
3rd DIVISION.

Vol 27

Confidential

War Diary

of

D.A.D.O.S   3rd Division

From 1-10-16 to 31-10-16

Army Form C. 2118.

WAR DIARY
or
INTELLIGENCE SUMMARY
(Erase heading not required.)

Instructions regarding War Diaries and Intelligence Summaries are contained in F. S. Regs., Part II. and the Staff Manual respectively. Title Pages will be prepared in manuscript.

Place	Date	Hour	Summary of Events and Information	Remarks and references to Appendices
BOMY	1/10/16		2 Trucks arrived including Bulk Clothing and Necessaries, 1500 Blankets etc.	D.A.D.O.S. 3rd DIVISION
BOMY	2/10/16		1 Truck General Stores, Pickling Soap, PH Helmets etc.	D.A.D.O.S. 3rd DIVISION
BOMY	3/10/16		1 Truck arrived including Bulk Clothing, Mubs, I Handles and Debot Stores	D.A.D.O.S. 3rd DIVISION
BOMY	4/10/16		1 Truck arrived including Bulk Sorks, Mineral Oil etc	D.A.D.O.S. 3rd DIVISION
BOMY	5/10/16		No stores arrived - Division a move South	D.A.D.O.S. 3rd DIVISION

Army Form C. 2118.

WAR DIARY
or
INTELLIGENCE SUMMARY

(Erase heading not required.)

Instructions regarding War Diaries and Intelligence Summaries are contained in F. S. Regs., Part II. and the Staff Manual respectively. Title Pages will be prepared in manuscript.

Place	Date	Hour	Summary of Events and Information	Remarks and references to Appendices
On Move South	6/10/16		No stores arrived	D.A.D.O.S. 3rd DIVISION
BERTRANCOURT (SOMME)	7/10		Arrived at BERTRANCOURT. Reserve Army, 5th Corps	D.A.D.O.S. 3rd DIVISION
BERTRANCOURT (SOMME)	8/10		No stores arrived. 250 Shelters obtained from 5th Corps and 300 Steel Helmets from 2nd Division	D.A.D.O.S. 3rd DIVISION
BERTRANCOURT (SOMME)	9/10		No stores arrived. 10 Tarpaulins obtained from 5th Corps	D.A.D.O.S. 3rd DIVISION
BERTRANCOURT (SOMME)	10/10		2 Trucks arrived containing stores from last Area. 30 Sets Tenth Button obtained from 5th Corps Troops	D.A.D.O.S. 3rd DIVISION

2449 Wt. W14957/M90 750,000 1/16 J.B.C. & A. Forms/C.2118/12.

Army Form C. 2118.

WAR DIARY
or
INTELLIGENCE SUMMARY

(Erase heading not required.)

Instructions regarding War Diaries and Intelligence Summaries are contained in F. S. Regs., Part II. and the Staff Manual respectively. Title Pages will be prepared in manuscript.

Place	Date	Hour	Summary of Events and Information	Remarks and references to Appendices
BERTRANCOURT	11/10		No stores arrived	D.A.D.O.S. 3rd DIVISION
BERTRANCOURT	12/10		1 Truck arrived from Rouen including Boots, Shoemaker Tools.	D.A.D.O.S. 3rd DIVISION
BERTRANCOURT	13/10		2 Trucks arrived including Bulk Picketing Gear, Oils, Soap, Clothing, Accoutrements, Horse Shoes, 900 Lewis Magazines, Paint, 1 Water Cart and 1 Limbered Wagon for Signals and 1 Water Cart for 23rd Battery.	D.A.D.O.S. 3rd DIVISION
BERTRANCOURT	14/10		2 Trucks arrived including Bulk Picketing Gear, Clothing, Soap, Horse Shoes, Lewis Magazines, Grenade Carriers, 77 9 Periscopes and 7020 Medical Cardigans to complete Infantry.	D.A.D.O.S. 3rd DIVISION
BERTRANCOURT	15/10		1 Truck arrived including Bulk Clothing, 6000 Socks and 4000 Cap Mackintosh, also General Stores	D.A.D.O.S. 3rd DIVISION

Army Form C. 2118.

WAR DIARY
or
INTELLIGENCE SUMMARY

(Erase heading not required.)

Instructions regarding War Diaries and Intelligence Summaries are contained in F.S. Regs., Part II. and the Staff Manual respectively. Title Pages will be prepared in manuscript.

Place	Date	Hour	Summary of Events and Information	Remarks and references to Appendices
BERTRANCOURT	16/10		1 Truck arrived including Bulk Clothing and Detail Stores	D.A.D.O.S. 3rd DIVISION
BERTRANCOURT	17/10		No Truck arrived	D.A.D.O.S. 3rd DIVISION
BERTRANCOURT 18/10 BUS les Artois			Truck arrived late at CONTEVILLE and could not be cleared owing to Move and great distance between Raikheim and Division. Division moved to BUS les Artois	D.A.D.O.S. 3rd DIVISION
BUS les Artois	19/10		2 Trucks arrived at Conteville showed to-day. General Stores and 2140& Boots, also 2 Jerseys for 12th W. Yorks {En5a05}	D.A.D.O.S. 3rd DIVISION
BUS les Artois	20/10		1 Truck arrived at ACHEUX including Bulk Petroling Gear & General Stores, 1500 Steel Helmets, 20 Very Pistols, 500 Blankets, 1792lbs Service Paint, 60 Electric Torches and 500 Sabulose for Smoke Helmets	D.A.D.O.S. 3rd DIVISION

WAR DIARY
or
INTELLIGENCE SUMMARY

(Erase heading not required.)

Army Form C. 2118.

Place	Date	Hour	Summary of Events and Information	Remarks and references to Appendices
BUS les ARTOIS	21/2/16		One Truck arrived including Bulk Oils, Soap, Grease, Accts. and Detail Stores	
BUS les ARTOIS	22/2/16		One Truck arrived including Bulk Clothing and Detail Stores, also General Hospital Clothing for A.D.M.S.	
BUS les ARTOIS	23/2/16		3 Trucks arrived today including Bulk Picketing and General Stores, 200 Brown, 13 T.M. Hand Carts, 1 18 Pr Gun Jr 10715y, 3 Lewis Guns for 13th Kings Liverpools, Bulk Horse Shoes and Stewart Tipping Machine.	
BUS les ARTOIS	24/2/16		2 Trucks arrived including 1500 Blankets, Bulk Socks Shirts, Necessaries and Shoemakers materials	
BUS les ARTOIS	25/2/16		No Stores arrived today. 75 Shelter obtained for Town Major from Corps Troops	

WAR DIARY
or
INTELLIGENCE SUMMARY
(Erase heading not required.)

Army Form C. 2118.

Place	Date	Hour	Summary of Events and Information	Remarks and references to Appendices
BUS les Artois	26/10/16		2 Trucks arrived including Bulk Boots (1450) Necessaries &c, also 1450 Horse Rugs, 40 Sets Packsaddlery. Received from 5th Div.	
BUS les Artois	27/10/16		2 Trucks arrived including Bulk Horse Shoes, 300 Brazier, 544 Canvas Magazine Covers, 100 Browse Bars and Detail Stores Art. 1 Gun Carriage for J.S.Bty R.F.A.	
BUS les Artois	28/10/16		No Truck arrived. 300 Steel Helmets received from 51st Div.	
BUS les Artois	29/10/16		1 Truck arrived including Bulk S.D. Clothing, 4200 Socks, etc. Leather Truck arrived including Bulk Camp Equipt, Picketing Gear &c.	
BUS les Artois	30/10/16		No stores arrived. 118 Soldiers obtained from O.O.C.1st Troop for R.A.	

Army Form C. 2118.

WAR DIARY
or
INTELLIGENCE SUMMARY
(Erase heading not required.)

Instructions regarding War Diaries and Intelligence Summaries are contained in F. S. Regs., Part II. and the Staff Manual respectively. Title Pages will be prepared in manuscript.

Place	Date	Hour	Summary of Events and Information	Remarks and references to Appendices
BVS in Antrim	3/1/16		One Truck arrived with 18 Pr Gun for 49th Battery, also 1 Truck Buck Blankets, Smoke Helmets &c and 1 VICKERS Gun for 9th M.G. Coy	B/S D.O.O. 3rd DIVISION

Percy Earp.
Captain

D.A.D.O.S.
3rd DIVISION.

WAR DIARY
or
INTELLIGENCE SUMMARY

Army Form C. 2118.

DADOS 3D
Vol 28

Place	Date	Hour	Summary of Events and Information	Remarks and references to Appendices
BUS les Artois	1/11		5 Trucks arrived including Bath Ankle Boots, F.S. Boots, Shirts, Drawers, Necessaries, Jerseys, Horse Rugs	DE
BUS les Artois	2/11		6 Trucks arrived including Bath Oils, Soap, Dubbing, Accoutrements, 12 Lewis Hand Carts, 3500 Blankets, 1 18 Pdr for 41st Battery 3 G.S. Limbered Wagons. 1 each 8th G.of, 76th M.G. Coy., 1 Water Cart for 149th Battery 3 G.S. Limbered Wagon for 4 Royal Irish.	DE
BUS les Artois	3/11		No Trucks today. Tents obtained from Town Major LOUVENCOURT	DE
BUS les Artois	4/11		3 Trucks arrived including Bath Horse Shoes, One 18 Pounder for 41st Battery, Bath Oils, Soap, Dubbing, Accoutrements, 40 Vermorel Sprayers, San Helmets and Shields, Etc.	DE
BUS les Artois	5/11		No Trucks arrived today	DE

Army Form C. 2118.

WAR DIARY
or
INTELLIGENCE SUMMARY

(Erase heading not required.)

Instructions regarding War Diaries and Intelligence Summaries are contained in F. S. Regs., Part II. and the Staff Manual respectively. Title Pages will be prepared in manuscript.

Place	Date	Hour	Summary of Events and Information	Remarks and references to Appendices
BUS les Artois	6/4/16		4 Trucks arrived including 8000 Shirts, 6000 Drawers, 3600 Body Bands, 18000 pieces Worsted, 800 Horse Rugs, 100 Brazien Picketing Gear &c. and 1 Lewis Gun for 12th W. Yorks. Bulk S.D. Clothing.	D.A.D.O.S. DIVISION. VE
BUS les Artois	7/4/16		4 Trucks arrived including Bulk Jerkin, Undercoats Fur. Coats 33 lined Caps, Socks, Towels, Drawers, 1225 Horse Rugs and 2 18 Pounder Guns, 1 each for 23rd and 108th Batteries.	D.A.D.O.S. DIVISION. VE
BUS les Artois	8/4/16		2 Trucks arrived including 1070 Boots Rubble, 180 Boots F.S., 16580 Sols. Inner 3000 Vests and 30 Scouts Overalls, also 1 18 Pr Carriage for 49th Battery Feather Truck with one 18 Pounder for 23rd Battery and 2 Wheels.	D.A.D.O.S. VE
BUS les Artois	9/4/16		One Truck arrived including Bulk Oils, Soap, Dubbing and General Stores also 1 18 Pr Carriage for 23rd Battery and 1 Vickers Gun for 8th M.G. Coy	VE
BUS les Artois	10/4/16		2 Trucks arrived including Bulk Horse Shoes, Detail Stores, 1 R.E. Limber for Jng. R.G. 1 Wagon S.S. and 1 Water Cart for 25th Battery	VE

Army Form C. 2118.

WAR DIARY
or
INTELLIGENCE SUMMARY

(Erase heading not required.)

Instructions regarding War Diaries and Intelligence Summaries are contained in F. S. Regs., Part II. and the Staff Manual respectively. Title Pages will be prepared in manuscript.

Place	Date	Hour	Summary of Events and Information	Remarks and references to Appendices
Bus les Artois	11/16		2 Trucks arrived including Bulk S.D Clothing, Scouts Overalls, 5000 Woollen Drawers and 12,000 Vest woollen	D.A.D.O.S., 3rd DIVISION. RE
Bus les Artois	12/16		1 Truck arrived including Bulk General Stores, Pickering Sean &c.	D.A.D.O.S., 3rd DIVISION. RE
Bus les Artois	13/16		No Stores arrived.	D.A.D.O.S., 3rd DIVISION. RE
Bus les Artois	14/16		No Stores arrived	D.A.D.O.S., 3rd DIVISION. RE
Bus les Artois	15/16		1 Truck arrived including 7900 Socks, Caps, Towels etc	D.A.D.O.S., 3rd DIVISION. RE

Army Form C. 2118.

WAR DIARY
or
INTELLIGENCE SUMMARY
(Erase heading not required.)

Instructions regarding War Diaries and Intelligence Summaries are contained in F.S. Regs., Part II. and the Staff Manual respectively. Title Pages will be prepared in manuscript.

Place	Date	Hour	Summary of Events and Information	Remarks and references to Appendices
BUS les Artois	16/11/16		2 Trucks arrived including 3 ny Lewis Gun, One 18 Pr pps 49th Battery, 1 Limber Body for 3/Brig. Coy. R.E. and 1 Pontoon Wagon for 56. Coy. R.E.	R.C.
BUS les Artois	17/11/16		One 18 Pr. Carriage received for 49th Battery also 2 Lewis Gun for 1/N.F. 9 Lewis Guns transferred to 31st Div. together with 5 released by Pioneer Battn.	J.E.
BUS les Artois	18/11/16		One Truck arrived including Bulk Horse Shoes, Oil, Soap, Acct &c. Also Truck with me Water Cart sent for 108th Brigade and D. How Bry and 1. G.S. Limbered Wagon for Pioneer Battn.	J.C.
BUS les Artois	19/11/16		3 Trucks arrived including Bulk Boots, S.D. Clothing, 3000 Vests, 4017 Leather Jerkins, Bulk Picketing and General Stores and 27 Wheels	J.E.
BUS les Artois	20/11/16		No Trucks today	

WAR DIARY or INTELLIGENCE SUMMARY

Army Form C. 2118.

Place	Date	Hour	Summary of Events and Information	Remarks and references to Appendices
BUS les Artois	21/11		1 Truck arrived including 4200 Socks, Towels, Caps, Haversacks, Spanners and Sundry Stores	D.A.D.O.S. 3rd DIVISION
BUS les Artois	22/11		5 Trucks arrived today, including 7000 Tangalin Covers, 1594 Jerkins, 4052 Inner Soles, Infirm Boots, 574 Boots, M.C. Clothing, and Chevrons & Badges, also One 18Pr & Carriage for 41st Battery. 1 Amm-Wagon 15Pr & Limber for 108th Bty. 1 Water Cart compt. for 29th Bty and 3 Coy Train and 2 R.E. Limbered Wagons for Bde Sig Coy R.E.	I.A.D.O.S. 3rd DIVISION
BUS les Artois	23/11		2 Trucks arrived including Bulk Oils, Soap, Grease, Lewis Magazines, 1 18Pr and Carriage for 108th Battery and 2 Maltese Carts for 3rd Coy R.E.	I.A.D.O.S. 3rd DIVISION
BUS les Artois	24/11		2 Trucks arrived each with 2400 Blankets	I.A.D.O.S. 3rd DIVISION
BUS les Artois	25/11		1 Truck arrived including Bulk Horse Shoes, Axles &c, also 1 Truck with S.D. Clothing, 2000 Drawers, M.C. Clothing &c	D.A.D.O.S. 3rd DIVISION

Army Form C. 2118.

WAR DIARY
or
INTELLIGENCE SUMMARY

(Erase heading not required.)

Instructions regarding War Diaries and Intelligence Summaries are contained in F. S. Regs., Part II. and the Staff Manual respectively. Title Pages will be prepared in manuscript.

Place	Date	Hour	Summary of Events and Information	Remarks and references to Appendices
BVS Les Pilars	26/11/16		No stores today	[D.A.D.O.S. 3rd DIVISION stamp]
BVS Les Pilars	27/11/16		2 Trucks arrived today including 1529 Leather Jerkins and 1000 Blankets	[D.A.D.O.S. 3rd DIVISION stamp]
BVS Les Pilars	28/11/16		3 Trucks arrived containing 5950 Blankets (Overdue Trucks)	[D.A.D.O.S. 3rd DIVISION stamp]
BVS Les Pilars	29/11/16		2 Trucks arrived including Bulk Nosebags, Dental Instructs; and 150 One respirator bags, also 1 Travn. Kitchen for Suffolks and 1 Limber Wagon for 9#MG Coy	[D.A.D.O.S. 3rd DIVISION stamp]
BVS Les Pilars	30/11/16		1 Truck arrived including Bulk Clothing and Boots, also Shoemakers Materials and 2 pr Gloves MT	[D.A.D.O.S. 3rd DIVISION stamp]

Reventa
Captain
D.A.D.O.S.
3rd DIVISION.
30/11/16

Vol 29

D.A.D.O.S.,
3rd DIVISION.

Confidential

War Diary

of

D.A.D.O.S. 3rd Division

From 1·12·16 to 31·12·16

Army Form C. 2118.

WAR DIARY
or
INTELLIGENCE SUMMARY
(Erase heading not required.)

Instructions regarding War Diaries and Intelligence Summaries are contained in F. S. Regs., Part II. and the Staff Manual respectively. Title Pages will be prepared in manuscript.

Place	Date	Hour	Summary of Events and Information	Remarks and references to Appendices
BUS les Artois	1/12/16		2 Trucks arrived including Bulk S.D. Clothing, Picketing Gear, 3000 Hay Nets, Oils, Soap &c, Necessaries &c, No.9 Printers for distribution, etc &c.	A.D.O.S. 1st DIVISION
BUS les Artois	2/12/16		1 Truck arrived including Bulk Horse Shoes, Dubbing, Soap &c, Saddlers and Details Stores, also 37 Wheels for Vehicles.	A.D.O.S. 2nd DIVISION
BUS les Artois	3/12/16		1 Truck arrived including Bulk Boots, 6000 Vests, 1500 Drawers Woollen, 255 Sweaters, also Running Out Springs in 7 to Air Truck.	A.D.O.S. 3rd DIVISION
Bus les Artois	4/12/16		No stores today	O.B. 3rd DIVISION
BUS les Artois	5/12/16		1 Truck arrived including Bulk Picketing Gear, General Stores and 10 Sayers Stoves and 200 Horse Rugs	O.B.

WAR DIARY
or
INTELLIGENCE SUMMARY

(Erase heading not required.)

Army Form C. 2118.

Place	Date	Hour	Summary of Events and Information	Remarks and references to Appendices
BHS les Artois	6/12/16		3 Trucks arrived including Bulk S.D. Clothing, Shirts, Socks, Drawers, Messingers, Shoemakers and Saddlers Stores, 19 T.M. Handcarts, 1 18Pr Gun and Carriage for 4 g/Mortars, 1 Mountain for 130th Battery and 1 Maltese Cart for Eng Sig. Coy.	
BHS les Artois	7/12/16		1 Truck arrived including Bulk Oils, Soft Accoutrements, 6.00 Blankets 10 Sayers Stoves, Wash, etc	
BHS les Artois	8/12/16		2 Trucks arrived including Bulk Horse Shoes, Boots, P.H. Helmets, Lewis Magazines, 11 Sayers Stoves, Straps for Gumboots, etc. &c.	
BHS les Artois	9/12/16		No stores today. 214 pairs Gum Boots rec'd from O/C Corps Tps to replace U. also 60 Brazier	
BHS les Artois	10/12/16		2 Trucks arrived including Bulk Picketing Gear, General Stores and 1 Lewis Gun for 1st R. Scots Fus.	

Army Form C. 2118

WAR DIARY
or
INTELLIGENCE SUMMARY
(Erase heading not required.)

Instructions regarding War Diaries and Intelligence Summaries are contained in F. S. Regs., Part II. and the Staff Manual respectively. Title Pages will be prepared in manuscript.

Place	Date	Hour	Summary of Events and Information	Remarks and references to Appendices
BUS les Artois	11/12/16		1 Truck arrived including 4800 Sapts, 1000 Shirts, 1000 Caps, Waistcoats, Caps, Towels, Necessaries, Gunmakers Materials &c	J.A.D.O.S., DIVISION. DE.
BUS les Artois	12/12/16		2 Trucks including 8140 Small Box Respirators and Detail Stores also 1 Truck with 2 Patterns for A Coy R.E.	J.A.D.O.S., DIVISION. DE.
BUS les Artois	13/12/16		2 Trucks arrived including Gick Boots and Small Box Respirators	J.A.D.O.S., DIVISION. DE.
BUS les Artois	14/12/16		1 Truck arrived including Bulk Oils, Dubbing, Soap, Accoutrements and 1860 Small Box Respirators	J.A.D.O.S., DIVISION. DE.
BUS les Artois	15/12/16		1 Truck arrived including Gick Horse Shoes, 1810 Small Box Respirators, Detail Stores and 1 18 Pr Gun for 29th Battery, also 1 Truck with Wor Cart for 29 By, Water Cart for 129 By and 15 Wheels	J.A.D.O.S., DIVISION. DE.

Army Form C. 2118.

WAR DIARY
or
INTELLIGENCE SUMMARY
(Erase heading not required.)

Instructions regarding War Diaries and Intelligence Summaries are contained in F. S. Regs., Part II. and the Staff Manual respectively. Title Pages will be prepared in manuscript.

Place	Date	Hour	Summary of Events and Information	Remarks and references to Appendices
BVS Les Artois	16/12/16		1 Truck arrived with 50 Sets Tent Bottoms	
BVS Les Artois	17/12/16		No Stores arrived today	
BVS Les Artois	18/12/16		1 Truck arrived including Duck Picketing Gear, Camp Equipt, and Dental Stores	
BVS Les Artois	19/12/16		No Stores today	
BVS Les Artois	20/12/16		2 Trucks arrived including Bell Boots, S.D. Clothing, Shirts, Socks etc &c. 500 Blankets obtained from Ord. Corps T/o	

Army Form C. 2118

WAR DIARY
or
INTELLIGENCE SUMMARY
(Erase heading not required.)

Instructions regarding War Diaries and Intelligence Summaries are contained in F. S. Regs., Part II. and the Staff Manual respectively. Title Pages will be prepared in manuscript.

Place	Date	Hour	Summary of Events and Information	Remarks and references to Appendices
BUS les Artois	21/12/16		1 Truck arrived including Vehicle Meals and Detail Stores	D.A.D.O.S., 8th Division
BUS les Artois	22/12/16		1 Truck arrived including Bulk Horse Shoes, Oil, Soap, and Respirators, P.H.Helmets	D.A.D.O.S., 8th Division
BUS les Artois	23/12/16		No Stores arriving	D.A.D.O.S., 8th Division
BUS les Artois	24/12/16		2 Trucks arrived including Bulk General Stores, Pickelinghaw, S.A. Dummy Cartgs and Detail Stores	A.D.O.S. 8th Division
BUS les Artois	25/12/16		1 Truck arrived including Bulk General Stores, Meals, and Detail Stores also 1870 Small Box Respirators	D.A.D.O.S., 8th Division

1875 Wt. W593/826 1,000,000 4/15 J.B.C. & A. A.D.S.S./Forms/C. 2118.

Army Form C. 2118

WAR DIARY
or
INTELLIGENCE SUMMARY
(Erase heading not required.)

Instructions regarding War Diaries and Intelligence Summaries are contained in F. S. Regs., Part II. and the Staff Manual respectively. Title Pages will be prepared in manuscript.

Place	Date	Hour	Summary of Events and Information	Remarks and references to Appendices
BUS les Artois	26/12/16		1 Truck arrived including Bulk Clothing, Detail Stores and 3300 prs Army Lambswool Socks	
BUS les Artois	27/12/16		3 Trucks arrived including Bulk Clothing, Boots, Necessaries, Showmakers Materials, 10 sets Marquee Bottoms, and 1 18Pr Gun Carriage for 108 Bty.	
BUS les Artois	28/12/16		No Stores arrived	
BUS les Artois	29/12/16		1 Truck arrived including Bulk Horse Shoes, Oils, Soap, &c.	
BUS les Artois	30/12/16		No Stores arrived	

Army Form C. 2118.

WAR DIARY
or
INTELLIGENCE SUMMARY.
(Erase heading not required.)

Instructions regarding War Diaries and Intelligence Summaries are contained in F. S. Regs., Part II. and the Staff Manual respectively. Title pages will be prepared in manuscript.

Place	Date	Hour	Summary of Events and Information	Remarks and references to Appendices
Bus les Artois	31/12/15		1 Truck arrived including Bulk General Stores, Picketing Gear, and Wagon Parts	D.A.D.O.S. 3rd DIVISION

3RD DIVISION
DIVL. TROOPS

DEP. ASST DIR. ORDNANCE SERVICES
JAN - DEC 1917.

Vol 30

Confidential

War Diary

of

DADVS 3rd Division

From 1-1-17 to 31-1-17

Army Form C. 2118.

WAR DIARY
or
INTELLIGENCE SUMMARY.
(Erase heading not required.)

Place	Date	Hour	Summary of Events and Information	Remarks and references to Appendices
BUS les Artois	1/1/17		No Stores today	
BUS les Artois	2/1/17		1 Truck arrived including Bulk Clothing and Detail Stores	
BUS les Artois	3/1/17		No Stores today except 3 G.S. Wagons for 1 Coy Div Train	
BUS les Artois	4/1/17		1 Truck today with 240 Horse Rugs	
BUS les Artois	5/1/17		No Stores today	

Army Form C. 2118.

WAR DIARY
or
INTELLIGENCE SUMMARY.
(Erase heading not required.)

Instructions regarding War Diaries and Intelligence Summaries are contained in F. S. Regs., Part II. and the Staff Manual respectively. Title pages will be prepared in manuscript.

Place	Date	Hour	Summary of Events and Information	Remarks and references to Appendices
Bus les Artois	6/7/17		6 Wheelers arrived today. Stores sent to Canaples	
Bus les Artois	7/7/17		No Stores today	
Bus les Artois CANAPLES	8/7/17		No Stores Today. Moved to CANAPLES	
CANAPLES	9/7/17		2 Trucks arrived including Bulk General and Detail Stores, Picketing Gear, Oil Soap &c, Plus and Wagon Exps and 52 Meals. Also 24 Lewis Guns, 2 each per Batt; making 12 per Batt.	
CANAPLES	10/7/17		One Truck arrived including 170 Horse Rugs	

2353 Wt.W2544/1154 700,000 5/15 D.D.&L. A.D.S.S.Forms/C.2118.

Army Form C. 2118.

WAR DIARY
or
INTELLIGENCE SUMMARY.
(Erase heading not required.)

Instructions regarding War Diaries and Intelligence Summaries are contained in F. S. Regs., Part II. and the Staff Manual respectively. Title pages will be prepared in manuscript.

Place	Date	Hour	Summary of Events and Information	Remarks and references to Appendices
CANAPLES	11/1/17		3 Trucks arrived including Bulk Boots, S.D. Clothing, Underclothing, and 1500 Copies Maintenance	D.A.D.O.S. 3rd DIVISION.
CANAPLES	12/1/17		1 Truck arrived including Bulk Oil, Soap, etc, Accts	D.A.D.O.S. 3rd DIVISION.
CANAPLES	13/1/17		1 Truck arrived including Bulk Horse Shoes, Detail Stores, Races, Packs etc etc	D.A.D.O.S. 3rd DIVISION.
CANAPLES	14/1/17		2 Trucks including Bulk General Stores, Picketing Gear, Clothing &c	D.A.D.O.S. 3rd DIVISION.
CANAPLES	15/1/17		2 Trucks arrived including Bulk S.D. Clothing, Underclothing, Necessaries and Sheepskin materials	D.A.D.O.S. 3rd DIVISION.

Army Form C. 2118.

WAR DIARY
or
INTELLIGENCE SUMMARY.
(Erase heading not required.)

Instructions regarding War Diaries and Intelligence Summaries are contained in F. S. Regs., Part II. and the Staff Manual respectively. Title pages will be prepared in manuscript.

Place	Date	Hour	Summary of Events and Information	Remarks and references to Appendices
CANAPLES	16/1/17		1 Truck arrived including Detail Stores and 27 Wheels	D.A.D.O.S., 3rd DIVISION.
CANAPLES	17/1/17		2 Trucks including Belt Boots, Clothing and Horse Rugs	D.A.D.O.S., 3rd DIVISION.
CANAPLES	18/1/17		No stores today	D.A.D.O.S., 3rd DIVISION.
CANAPLES	19/1/17		1 Truck arrived including Bulk Oils, Soap, Accts and Detail Stores	D.A.D.O.S., 3rd DIVISION.
CANAPLES	20/1/17		2 Trucks arrived including Bulk Horse Shoes and 30 Wheels	D.A.D.O.S., 3rd DIVISION.

2353 Wt. W2544/1454 700,000 5/15 D. D. & L. A.D.S.S.Form/C 2118.

Army Form C. 2118.

WAR DIARY
or
INTELLIGENCE SUMMARY.
(Erase heading not required.)

Place	Date	Hour	Summary of Events and Information	Remarks and references to Appendices
CANAPLES	21/7		2 Trucks arrived including Bulk Clothing, 3000 Shirts, 3000 Socks, 1 Waterproof 13th Lanciers, 1 Wagon limber body 2 for S.A.A. complete limbered Wagon 2/Rl Scots and 1 18 Pr for 59th Battery	D.A.D.O.S., 3rd DIVISION.
CANAPLES	22/7		5 Trucks arrived including Bulk General Stores, Mules, Pecking Gear and 14 Mark II Wagon limbers for R.H. &repiece Mark I	D.A.D.O.S., 3rd DIVISION.
CANAPLES	23/7		1 Truck arrived including Bulk Clothing &c	D.A.D.O.S., 3rd DIVISION.
CANAPLES	24/7		9 Trucks arrived including Petrol Stores, 50 Wheels, 31 Wagon limbers, 5 carriage limbers in exchange for Mark I, 1 Ammr Wagon for 129th Battery and 1 Ammr Wagon for 49th Battery	D.A.D.O.S., 3rd DIVISION.
CANAPLES	25/7		1 Truck arrived including Bulk Clothing, Shirts, Socks, Vests, Boots &c	D.A.D.O.S., 3rd DIVISION.

Army Form C. 2118.

WAR DIARY
or
INTELLIGENCE SUMMARY.
(Erase heading not required.)

Instructions regarding War Diaries and Intelligence Summaries are contained in F. S. Regs., Part II. and the Staff Manual respectively. Title pages will be prepared in manuscript.

Place	Date	Hour	Summary of Events and Information	Remarks and references to Appendices
CANAPLES	26/1/17		2 Trucks arrived including Bulk Oil Soap &c, 500 Blankets, 1 Vickers Gun for 8th M.G. Coy and 3 carriage trucks - Mk I in exchange of Mk I.	D.A.D.O.S., 3rd DIVISION. No........ Date........
CANAPLES	27/1/17		1 Truck arrived including Bulk Horse Shoes and Box refilling	D.A.D.O.S., 3rd DIVISION. No........ Date........
CANAPLES	28/1/17		No Stores arrived	D.A.D.O.S., 3rd DIVISION. No........ Date........
CANAPLES Third Army	29/1/17		No Stores. Division moved to Third Army	D.A.D.O.S., 3rd DIVISION. No........ Date........
Third Army On Move	30/1/17		No Stores. On Move	D.A.D.O.S., 3rd DIVISION. No........ Date........

Army Form C.2118.

WAR DIARY
or
INTELLIGENCE SUMMARY.

(Erase heading not required.)

Instructions regarding War Diaries and Intelligence Summaries are contained in F. S. Regs., Part II. and the Staff Manual respectively. Title pages will be prepared in manuscript.

Place	Date	Hour	Summary of Events and Information	Remarks and references to Appendices
VILLERS CHATEL	31/1/17		No Trucks. Wood stores from Canaples	D.A.D.O.S., 3rd DIVISION.

Steverfarp.
D.A.D.O.S.
3rd DIVISION.

Confidential

War Diary

of

D.A.D.O.S. 3rd Division

From 1-2-17 to 28-2-17

Army Form C. 2118.

WAR DIARY
or
INTELLIGENCE SUMMARY.
(Erase heading not required.)

Place	Date	Hour	Summary of Events and Information	Remarks and references to Appendices
VILLERS CHATEL	2/2/17		4 Trucks arrived. General Stores, Blankets, Whale Wagon Grease &c.	D.A.D.O.S., 3rd DIVISION.
VILLERS CHATEL	3/2/17		Truck from CANAPLES being cleared	D.A.D.O.S., 3rd DIVISION.
VILLERS CHATEL	4/2/17		Stores at Railhead all cleared. Stores sent out to units.	D.A.D.O.S., 3rd DIVISION.
VILLERS CHATEL	5/2/17		No Trucks today. Stores sent out to Units by Lorry.	D.A.D.O.S., 3rd DIVISION.
VILLERS CHATEL	6/2/17		No Truck today. Stores sent to Walters	D.A.D.O.S., 3rd DIVISION.

Army Form C. 2118.

WAR DIARY
or
INTELLIGENCE SUMMARY.
(Erase heading not required.)

Instructions regarding War Diaries and Intelligence Summaries are contained in F. S. Regs., Part II. and the Staff Manual respectively. Title pages will be prepared in manuscript.

Place	Date	Hour	Summary of Events and Information	Remarks and references to Appendices
Villers Chatel	7/2/17		No Trucks today. Stores sent to Warlus and Ligneruil	D.A.D.O.S., 3rd DIVISION.
Villers Chatel	8/2/17		No Stores arrived. Moved to Ligneruil	D.A.D.O.S., 3rd DIVISION.
LIGERNEUIL	9/2/17		3 Trucks arrived - Clothing, General Stores, Steel Helmets, Door Respirators, Foot Logs, Nails etc	D.A.D.O.S., 3rd DIVISION.
LIGERNEUIL	10/2/17		1 Truck Horse Rugs arrived	D.A.D.O.S., 3rd DIVISION.
LIGERNEUIL WAPLUS	11/2/17		1 Truck Horse Shoes arrived	D.A.D.O.S., 3rd DIVISION.

Army Form C. 2118.

WAR DIARY
or
INTELLIGENCE SUMMARY.
(Erase heading not required.)

Instructions regarding War Diaries and Intelligence Summaries are contained in F.S. Regs., Part II. and the Staff Manual respectively. Title pages will be prepared in manuscript.

Place	Date	Hour	Summary of Events and Information	Remarks and references to Appendices
Warlus	12/2/17		1 Truck arrived including Buck Dubbing Soap, Ack & Detail Stores	D.A.D.O.S. 3rd DIVISION
WARLUS	13/2/17		1 Truck arrived including Buck General Stores, Rifle Cover, Fenin Magazines etc, also 1 Iron Kitchen Dixby for 8 Kings Own	D.A.D.O.S. 3rd DIVISION
WARLUS	14/2/17		1 Truck arrived including Buck Boots, Clothing, Packeting Gear &c	D.A.D.O.S. 3rd DIVISION
WARLUS	15/2/17		1 Truck arrived including 29 Snipers Stores. DDOS Third Army visited dump	D.A.D.O.S. 3rd DIVISION
WARLUS	16/2/17		Captain J.P. Best A.O.D. left for Annalls Clearing Station with view to proceeding to England. 2 Trucks stores arrived, 3000 Changes U.C., 2000 Socks, 116 Boxes Horse Shoes, Detail Stores and 1 Lewis Gun for Training purposes	D.A.D. 3rd DIVISION

Army Form C. 2118.

WAR DIARY
or
INTELLIGENCE SUMMARY.
(Erase heading not required.)

Instructions regarding War Diaries and Intelligence Summaries are contained in F. S. Regs., Part II. and the Staff Manual respectively. Title pages will be prepared in manuscript.

Place	Date	Hour	Summary of Events and Information	Remarks and references to Appendices
WARLUS	17/2/17		One Truck arrived with Mess Cart and 8th Kings Regt & Gordons and 1 complete Reserve Wagon for 1st R. Scots Fus.	D.A.D.O.S., 3rd Division
WARLUS	18/2/17		1 Truck arrived with 6 Tons General Stores, Oil, Soap, Pickling Jars &c, and one 4.5 Howitzer for 129th Battery. Road Precautions and Stores dumped at Station.	D.A.D.O.S., 3rd Division
WARLUS	19/2/17		No Trucks today.	D.A.D.O.S., 3rd Division
WARLUS	20/2/17		1 Truck arrived with 5 Tons General Stores, including 22 Lewis Guns to complete 18" to 14 each (except Pioneer 18"), also 150 Stretchers and 300 Blankets for A.D.M.S.	D.A.D.O.S., 3rd Division
WARLUS	21/2/17		1 Truck arrived including Boots, Clothing, Gas Appliances, Dental Stores &c	D.A.D.O.S., 3rd Division

Army Form C. 2118.

WAR DIARY
or
INTELLIGENCE SUMMARY.
(Erase heading not required.)

Place	Date	Hour	Summary of Events and Information	Remarks and references to Appendices
WARLUS	22/2/17		No Trucks arrived	
WARLUS	23/2/17		No Trucks arrived	
WARLUS	24/2/17		No Trucks arrived	
WARLUS	25/2/17		No Trucks arrived	
WARLUS	26/2/17		No Trucks arrived. Stores dumped at Station removed to Warlus	
WARLUS	27/2/17		4 Trucks arrived, also 1 Truck with Water Cart for 37 Coy R.E. 3 945 with T. Watson also received	

Army Form C. 2118.

WAR DIARY
or
INTELLIGENCE SUMMARY.
(Erase heading not required.)

Instructions regarding War Diaries and Intelligence Summaries are contained in F. S. Regs., Part II. and the Staff Manual respectively. Title pages will be prepared in manuscript.

Place	Date	Hour	Summary of Events and Information	Remarks and references to Appendices
WARLUS	28/2/17		2 Trucks arrived — 10 Tons. Taken to dump at Liencourt.	D.A.D.O.S., 3rd DIVISION.

Munro
Comr.

D.A.D.O.S., 3rd DIVISION.
A in H.

Vol. 32.

Confidential

War Diary

D.A.D.O.S. 3rd Division

From 1/3/17 to 31/3/17

Army Form C. 2118.

WAR DIARY
or
INTELLIGENCE SUMMARY.

(Erase heading not required.)

Instructions regarding War Diaries and Intelligence Summaries are contained in F. S. Regs., Part II. and the Staff Manual respectively. Title pages will be prepared in manuscript.

Place	Date	Hour	Summary of Events and Information	Remarks and references to Appendices
WARLUS	1/3/17		No Trucks arrived	D.A.D.O.S. 3rd DIVISION
WARLUS	2/3/17		1 Truck arrived, 700 Blankets and 335 Horse Rugs	D.A.D.O.S. 3rd DIVISION
WARLUS	3/3/17		1 Truck arrived - 9 Tor Snow Shoes, also 1 18 Pr Carriage for 41st Battery R.F.A.	D.A.D.O.S. 3rd DIVISION
WARLUS	4/3/17		2 Trucks arrived. Oils, Soap, Oats &c	D.A.D.O.S. 3rd DIVISION
WARLUS	5/3/17		No Stores arrived today. Lieut D.S. Jack arrived for duty vice Capt. Carp.	
WARLUS	6/3/17		1 Truck arrived. Petrol and Sound Stores. Also 100 Sets Packsaddles	

Army Form C. 2118.

WAR DIARY
or
INTELLIGENCE SUMMARY.

(Erase heading not required.)

Place	Date	Hour	Summary of Events and Information	Remarks and references to Appendices
WARLUS	7/7/17		1 Truck from Stores, Boots &c	D.A.D.O.S. 3rd DIVISION
WARLUS	8/7/17		No stores to-day. Shortage of Boots, Grinding and Shoemakers Tools &c. Matter referred to A.D.O.S. H.Q.	D.A.D.O.S. 3rd DIVISION
WARLUS	9/7/17		1 Truck arrived - 9 Tons Horse Shoes, Clothing &c	
WARLUS	10/7/17		3 Trucks arrived with 2 limbered Wagons for Hedeni R.E and one Travelling Kitchen for 1st Gordons	D.A.D.O.S 3rd DIVISION
WARLUS	11/7/17		2 Trucks arrived General Stores and Clothing &	D.A.D.O.S. 3rd DIVISION

Army Form C. 2118.

WAR DIARY
or
INTELLIGENCE SUMMARY.
(Erase heading not required.)

Instructions regarding War Diaries and Intelligence Summaries are contained in F. S. Regs., Part II. and the Staff Manual respectively. Title pages will be prepared in manuscript.

Place	Date	Hour	Summary of Events and Information	Remarks and references to Appendices
WARLUS	13/7/17		2 Trucks arrived	
WARLUS	14/3/17		1 Truck arrived containing box Respirators &c.	
WARLUS	14/3/17		4 Trucks arrived. General Stores, Packsaddlery, M.G. Chests, and 5 Ton Boats, also 1 G.S. Wagon for 2. Sect. 3.70.A.C. Dumps formed at TINQUES	
WARLUS	15/3/17		3 Trucks arrived. 1 Motor Cart for 6th Battery, 2 Wagon Ammn each for 6th, 23rd and 49th Batteries	
WARLUS	16/3/17		2 Trucks arrived. Horse Shoes, Clothing, General and Detail Stores 25 Wheels and 1 Malline Cart for 142. Fd Amb	
WARLUS	17/3/17		No Trucks arrived. TINQUES Dump being cleared	

2353 Wt. W2544/1451 700,000 5/15 D. D. & L. A.D.S.S.Forms/C. 2118.

Army Form C. 2118.

WAR DIARY
or
INTELLIGENCE SUMMARY.
(Erase heading not required.)

Instructions regarding War Diaries and Intelligence Summaries are contained in F. S. Regs., Part II. and the Staff Manual respectively. Title pages will be prepared in manuscript.

Place	Date	Hour	Summary of Events and Information	Remarks and references to Appendices
WARLUS	18/3/17		2 Trucks arrived. Accts, Ord, Soap &c. Services, Camp Equipt &c, also 1 Water Cart for Cheshire R.E. Coy	D.A.D.O.S. 3rd DIVISION.
WARLUS	19/3/17		No Trucks today	D.A.D.O.S. 3rd DIVISION.
WARLUS	20/3/17		2 Trucks arrived. General Stores, P.H. Helmets, 300 Boxes Tin for Magazines and 3000 Changes Underclothing	D.A.D.O.S. 3rd DIVISION.
WARLUS	21/3/17		1 Truck arrived. Clothing, Boots and General Stores	D.A.D.O.S. 3rd DIVISION.
WARLUS	22/3/17		No stores today	D.A.D.O.S. 3rd DIVISION.

WAR DIARY
or
INTELLIGENCE SUMMARY

Army Form C. 2118.

Place	Date	Hour	Summary of Events and Information	Remarks and references to Appendices
WARLUS	23/7/17		1 Truck arrived with 2 Horse Shoes Pads, clothing, necessaries etc, also 1 Lewis Gun for 8th E. Yorks	
WARLUS	24/7/17		No Truck arrived. Lorries used for taking up Reserve Stores to Area.	
WARLUS	25/7/17		1 Truck General Stores, Rivets, R.E. Dubbing &c	
WARLUS	26/7/17		1 Truck arrived with 1 Limbered G.S. Wagon for 1/Sect. 3 DFC, and from 9"/45" Trench Mortars. Trench Mortars taken to Arras.	
WARLUS	27/7/17		No Truck arrived. Lorries sent to Raithan & clean Heavy T.M. Amm. Lost R.T.O. but Head Army wrote to hand over to 17 Corp.	

Army Form C. 2118.

WAR DIARY
or
INTELLIGENCE SUMMARY.
(Erase heading not required.)

Instructions regarding War Diaries and Intelligence Summaries are contained in F. S. Regs., Part II. and the Staff Manual respectively. Title pages will be prepared in manuscript.

Place	Date	Hour	Summary of Events and Information	Remarks and references to Appendices
WARLUS	28/3/17		D.D.O.S. This Hwn visited Dump. No Trucks arrived	D.A.D.O.S. 3rd DIVISION.
WARLUS	29/3/17		2 Trucks arrived. Boots, Clothing, General Stores &c, also one 18Pr Gun 23rd Battery R.F.A.	D.A.D.O.S. 3rd DIVISION.
WARLUS	30/3/17		No Trucks arrived. 1 Truck advised	D.A.D.O.S. 3rd DIVISION.
WARLUS	31/3/17		No Trucks arrived. 2 Trucks advised. 18 Pounder Gun Barrel No 1858 - 49th Battery and 4.5" How Barrel - 129th Battery sent to Base in Truck 159151	A.D.O.S. 3rd DIVISION.

D.A.D.O.S. 3rd DIVISION.

Vol 33

Confidential WAR DIARY

D.A.D.O.S 3rd Div

Period 1-4-17 to 30-4-17

Army Form C. 2118.

WAR DIARY
or
INTELLIGENCE SUMMARY.
(Erase heading not required.)

Place	Date	Hour	Summary of Events and Information	Remarks and references to Appendices
WARLUS	1/4/17		No Trucks arrived. Two 2 und T.M. demanded, one each for Y & Z. T.M. Bys.	D.A.D.O.S. 3rd DIVISION [stamp/signature]
WARLUS	2/4/17		No Trucks arrived. 11 G.S. limbered Wagons taken over by Div. B. employed from M.G. Transport	D.A.D.O.S. 3rd DIVISION [stamp/signature]
WARLUS	3/4/17		2 Trucks arrived, General Stores, Underclothing, Grinding & Mecanien etc.	D.A.D.O.S. 3rd DIVISION [stamp/signature]
WARLUS	4/4/17		No stores arrived. Lorries used on various work, Petrol Tins collecting stores from Corps Base	D.A.D.O.S. 3rd DIVISION [stamp/signature]
WARLUS	5/4/17		No stores arrived. Lorries employed clearing Salvage to Railhead	D.A.D.O.S. 3rd DIVISION [stamp/signature]

Army Form C. 2118.

WAR DIARY
or
INTELLIGENCE SUMMARY.
(Erase heading not required.)

Instructions regarding War Diaries and Intelligence Summaries are contained in F. S. Regs., Part II. and the Staff Manual respectively. Title pages will be prepared in manuscript.

Place	Date	Hour	Summary of Events and Information	Remarks and references to Appendices
WARLUS	7/4/17		1 Truck arrived. 1830 Blankets, General Stores, Three 2" T.M. and One Lewis Gun for 12th W. Yorks	D.A.D.O.S. 3rd DIVISION.
WARLUS	9/4/17		1 Truck Clothing &c	D.A.D.O.S. 3rd DIVISION.
WARLUS	9/4/17		1 Truck arrived Box'k Horse Shoes, Camp Equipt General Stores &c	D.A.D.O.S. 3rd DIVISION.
WARLUS	10/4/17		No stores arrived	D.A.D.O.S. 3rd DIVISION.
WARLUS ARRAS	11/4/17		1 Truck arrived Petrolting Saws, Detail Stores &c, also 2 Trucks with 4 Travn Kitchens for 7th Shrops L.I.	D.A.D.O.S. 3rd DIVISION.

Army Form C. 2118.

WAR DIARY
or
INTELLIGENCE SUMMARY.
(Erase heading not required.)

Place	Date	Hour	Summary of Events and Information	Remarks and references to Appendices
WARLUS ARRAS	12/4/17		No Stores arrived	D.A.D.O.S., 3rd DIVISION
WARLUS ARRAS	13/4/17		1 G.S. Wagon arrived from 2/Seat. 3rd D.A.C.	D.A.D.O.S., 3rd DIVISION
WARLUS ARRAS	14/4/17		3 Trucks arrived. Clothing, General Stores &c	D.A.D.O.S., 3rd DIVISION
WARLUS ARRAS	15/4/17		1 Truck General Stores etc, also 1 Stokes gun for 8th M.Bty	D.A.D.O.S., 3rd DIVISION
WARLUS ARRAS	16/4/17		No Stores arrived. Lorries clearing Winter Clothing &c	D.A.D.O.S., 3rd DIVISION
WARLUS ARRAS	17/4/17		No Stores arrived. Lorries clearing Winter Clothing &c	D.A.D.O.S., 3rd DIVISION

Army Form C. 2118.

WAR DIARY
or
INTELLIGENCE SUMMARY.
(Erase heading not required.)

Instructions regarding War Diaries and Intelligence Summaries are contained in F. S. Regs., Part II. and the Staff Manual respectively. Title pages will be prepared in manuscript.

Place	Date	Hour	Summary of Events and Information	Remarks and references to Appendices
WARLUS	18/4/17		No stores today. Lorries drawing Winter Clothing	
WARLUS	19/4/17		1 Truck arrived, Oils Paints &c, Wheels and General Stores	
WARLUS	20/4/17		2 Trucks arrived, Horse Shoes &c, and 1 Trav. Kitchen for 13th Kings Liverpools.	
WARLUS	21/4/17		No stores arrived	
WARLUS	22/4/17		No stores arrived, Lorries drawing Winter Clothing	

Army Form C. 2118.

WAR DIARY
or
INTELLIGENCE SUMMARY.
(Erase heading not required.)

Instructions regarding War Diaries and Intelligence Summaries are contained in F. S. Regs., Part II. and the Staff Manual respectively. Title pages will be prepared in manuscript.

Place	Date	Hour	Summary of Events and Information	Remarks and references to Appendices
WARLUS ARRAS	23/4/17		1 Truck arrived with Water Cart for 7th Shrops L.I. and 12 T.M. Handcarts	D.A.D.O.S.
WARLUS ARRAS	24/4/17		2 Trucks arrived. Several Stores Petrol etc Sgn. Box Respirators etc. and 3 Kroun Wagons, 1 each for 1 Sct DAC, 23rd & 129.4th Bn	D.A.D.O. 3rd Divn
WARLUS ARRAS	25/4/17		Moved Dumps and Office to Arras. 30 Tons Clothing arrived	D.A.D.O.S. 3rd Divn
WARLUS ARRAS	26/4/17		No Trucks arrived	D.A.D.O.S. 3rd DIVISION
WARLUS ARRAS	27/4/17		1 Truck. Horse Shoes, Oil, Soap, Dubbing, Box Respirator	D.A.D.O.S. 3rd DIVISION

Army Form C. 2118.

WAR DIARY
or
INTELLIGENCE SUMMARY.
(Erase heading not required.)

Instructions regarding War Diaries and Intelligence Summaries are contained in F. S. Regs., Part II. and the Staff Manual respectively. Title pages will be prepared in manuscript.

Place	Date	Hour	Summary of Events and Information	Remarks and references to Appendices
ARRAS	28/4/17		No Trucks	D.A.D.O.S., 3rd Division
ARRAS	29/4/17		1 Truck, 1 Ton Clothing. 5 Wagon Pain for 6" Battery. Moved offices and dumps. 4 T.M. 2 inch J. Trs.	D.A.D.O.S., 3rd Division
ARRAS	30/4/17		1 Truck General Stores	D.A.D.O.S., 3rd Division

Dyer, Lieut
D.A.D.O.S.,
3rd Division.

Vol 34

Confidential War Diary

D.A.D.O.S. 3rd Division

from 1-5-17 to 31-5-17

Army Form C. 2118.

WAR DIARY
or
INTELLIGENCE SUMMARY.
(Erase heading not required.)

Place	Date	Hour	Summary of Events and Information	Remarks and references to Appendices
ARRAS	1/5/17		No Trucks arrived. 3 Lorries Stores rec'd from 29th Div for Units attached.	
ARRAS	2/5/17		No Trucks arrived	
ARRAS	3/5/17		2 Trucks arrived. Clothing, Boots, General Stores, 1500 Horse Respirators	
ARRAS	4/5/17		No Trucks arrived	
ARRAS	5/5/17		No Trucks arrived	

WAR DIARY
or
INTELLIGENCE SUMMARY.
(Erase heading not required.)

Army Form C. 2118.

Place	Date	Hour	Summary of Events and Information	Remarks and references to Appendices
ARRAS	6/5/17		2 Trucks arrived. S.D. Clothing &c. Also 1 Mess Cart for 92 Bdy and 1 Limbered Wagon for N.Z. Tunn. Coy	D.A.D.O.S., 3rd DIVISION.
ARRAS	7/5/17		1 Truck arrived. Horseshoes and General Stores. Also Truck with G.S. Wagon for 256 K.R.R.	D.A.D.O.S., 3rd DIVISION.
ARRAS	8/5/17		1 Truck General Stores.	
ARRAS	9/5/17		3 Trucks arrived. 11 Tons Boots & Clothing, Vehicles &c	D.A.D.O.S., 3rd DIVISION.
ARRAS	10/5/17		No Trucks arrived	D.A.D.O.S., 3rd DIVISION.

Army Form C. 2118.

WAR DIARY
or
INTELLIGENCE SUMMARY.
(Erase heading not required.)

Instructions regarding War Diaries and Intelligence Summaries are contained in F. S. Regs., Part II. and the Staff Manual respectively. Title pages will be prepared in manuscript.

Place	Date	Hour	Summary of Events and Information	Remarks and references to Appendices
ARRAS	11/5/17		4 Trucks arrived, General Stores, Oils, Bedding, Soap &c., Horse Shoes, etc., also 3 Ammn Wagons 23rd Battery, and 2 limbers Ammn Wagon 29th Battery	D.A.D.O.S. 3rd DIVISION
ARRAS	12/5/17		1 Truck clothing arrived	D.A.D.O.S. 3rd DIVISION
ARRAS	13/5/17		1 Truck General Stores	D.A.D.O.S. 3rd DIVISION
ARRAS	14/5/17		No Trucks arrived	D.A.D.O.S. 3rd DIVISION
ARRAS WARLUS	15/5/17		1 Truck General Stores, Moved to Warlus	D.A.D.O.S. 3rd DIVISION
WARLUS	16/5/17		1 Truck arrived, Boots & Clothing	D.A.D.O.S. 3rd DIVISION

Army Form C. 2118.

WAR DIARY
or
INTELLIGENCE SUMMARY.
(Erase heading not required.)

Instructions regarding War Diaries and Intelligence Summaries are contained in F. S. Regs., Part II. and the Staff Manual respectively. Title pages will be prepared in manuscript.

Place	Date	Hour	Summary of Events and Information	Remarks and references to Appendices
WARLUS	17/5/17		No Truck arrived	D.A.D.O.S., 3rd DIVISION.
WARLUS	18/5/17		1 Truck arrived, Horse Shoes, Oils, Soap &c.	D.A.D.O.S., 3rd DIVISION.
WARLUS	19/5/17		1 Truck arrived, Clothing &c. Moved to LIGNEREUIL	D.A.D.O.S., 3rd DIVISION.
LIGNEREUIL	20/5/17		No Stores arrived	D.A.D.O.S., 3rd DIVISION.
LIGNEREUIL	21/5/17		1 Truck arrived, Issued & Detail Stores	D.A.D.O.S., 3rd DIVISION.
LIGNEREUIL	22/5/17		No Stores. Issued Remaining Clothing	D.A.D.O.S., 3rd DIVISION.

Army Form C. 2118.

WAR DIARY
or
INTELLIGENCE SUMMARY.
(Erase heading not required.)

Instructions regarding War Diaries and Intelligence Summaries are contained in F. S. Regs., Part II. and the Staff Manual respectively. Title pages will be prepared in manuscript.

Place	Date	Hour	Summary of Events and Information	Remarks and references to Appendices
LIGNEREUIL	23/5/17		No Stores today. Lorries clearing Old Clothing, and delivering stores to R.A. at Frevent	D.A.D.O.S., 3rd DIVISION.
LIGNEREUIL	24/5/17		2 Trucks arrived. General Stores, Clothing &c	D.A.D.O.S., 3rd DIVISION.
LIGNEREUIL	25/5/17		No Trucks. Stores sent to Artillery at Arras and to 57 & 76 F.A. at St Pol	D.A.D.O.S.
LIGNEREUIL	26/5/17		1 Truck arrived Clothing &c	D.A.D.O.S.
LIGNEREUIL	27/5/17		1 Truck arrived	
LIGNEREUIL	28/5/17		No stores arrived. Gun Spares collected from Frevent	D.A.D.O.S., 3rd DIVISION.

Army Form C. 2118.

WAR DIARY
or
INTELLIGENCE SUMMARY.
(Erase heading not required.)

Instructions regarding War Diaries and Intelligence Summaries are contained in F. S. Regs., Part II. and the Staff Manual respectively. Title pages will be prepared in manuscript.

Place	Date	Hour	Summary of Events and Information	Remarks and references to Appendices
LIGNEREUIL	29/5		1 Truck arrived, Clothing &c.	D.A.D.O.S., 3rd DIVISION.
LIGNEREUIL	30/5		1 Truck arrived, General Stores &c. Stores sent to Pars. for R.A. Units	D.A.D.O.S., 3rd DIVISION.
LIGNEREUIL	31/5		1 Truck arrived, General Stores, Oil, Soap &c	D.A.D.O.S., 3rd DIVISION.

D.J. Jack, Captain
D.A.D.O.S., 3rd DIVISION.

Secret

Vol 35

War Diary

D.A.D.O.S
3rd Division
Captⁿ D J JACK. AOD

From 1 6 17
To 30 6 17

J.J.Jack, Captain

D.A.D.O.S.,
3rd DIVISION.
No. 1717

D.A.D.O.S
3rd Echelon
Base

War Diary for period 1.6.17 to 30.6.17 is forwarded herewith please

A.S. Jack. Captain

D.A.D.O.S.,
3rd DIVISION.

Army Form C. 2118.

WAR DIARY
or
INTELLIGENCE SUMMARY.
(Erase heading not required.)

Instructions regarding War Diaries and Intelligence Summaries are contained in F. S. Regs., Part II. and the Staff Manual respectively. Title pages will be prepared in manuscript.

Place	Date	Hour	Summary of Events and Information	Remarks and references to Appendices
LIGNEREUIL	1/6/17		1 Truck arrived. Horse Shoes and General Stores	D.A.D.O.S. 3rd DIVISION.
LIGNEREUIL	2/6/17		1 Truck - Clothing &c., Moved to Arras	D.A.D.O.S. 3rd DIVISION.
ARRAS	3/6/17		No Stores. Moved Dump again in Arras	D.A.D.O.S. 3rd DIVISION.
ARRAS	4/6/17		1 Truck arrived - General Stores	D.A.D.O.S. 3rd DIVISION.
ARRAS	5/6/17		No Stores arrived.	D.A.D.O.S. 3rd DIVISION.
ARRAS	6/6/17		1 Truck arrived, Clothing &c., also Mules from Rouen	D.A.D.O.S. 3rd DIVISION.

WAR DIARY
or
INTELLIGENCE SUMMARY.

Army Form C. 2118.

Place	Date	Hour	Summary of Events and Information	Remarks and references to Appendices
Arras	7/6/17		No stores arrived	D.A.D.O.S., 3rd DIVISION
Arras	8/6/17		One Truck, Walter Cart for 13th Kings, 1 Water Cart for 41st Bty, and 1 Mess Cart for B/15 top R.H.A. Stores received for 29th Div R.E.	D.A.D.O.S., 3rd DIVISION
ARRAS	9/6/17		No stores arrived	D.A.D.O.S., 3rd DIVISION
ARRAS	10/6/17		3 Trucks arrived, Clothing and General Stores	D.A.D.O.S., 3rd DIVISION
ARRAS	11/6/17		No Trucks arrived	D.A.D.O.S., 3rd DIVISION

Army Form C. 2118.

WAR DIARY
or
INTELLIGENCE SUMMARY.
(Erase heading not required.)

Instructions regarding War Diaries and Intelligence Summaries are contained in F.S. Regs., Part II and the Staff Manual respectively. Title pages will be prepared in manuscript.

Place	Date	Hour	Summary of Events and Information	Remarks and references to Appendices
ARRAS	19/6	9.10pm	N° 8564 Conductor D. Murray A.O.C. Chief Clerk to DADOS 3/Div. Killed by Hostile Shell fire.	D.A.D.O.S., 3rd DIVISION.
			No Trucks arrived.	
ARRAS	13/6		2 Trucks arrived. 1 Math. Equip? & Gen. Stores & 1 with Wheels viz - 1 hats Cart for 130th Batt. 11 Kitchen Travelling Body for S/KORL N. Sam. Cond? Record N.G. Tools tree cloths of Chief Clerk.	D.A.D.O.S., 3rd DIVISION.
ARRAS	14/6		1 Truck . Clothing & Necessaries arrived	D.A.D.O.S., 3rd DIVISION.
ARRAS	15/6		No Trucks arrived. Stores clearing Old Clothing &c. to Railhead	D.A.D.O.S., 3rd DIVISION.

Army Form C. 2118.

WAR DIARY
or
INTELLIGENCE SUMMARY.
(Erase heading not required.)

Instructions regarding War Diaries and Intelligence Summaries are contained in F. S. Regs., Part II. and the Staff Manual respectively. Title pages will be prepared in manuscript.

Place	Date	Hour	Summary of Events and Information	Remarks and references to Appendices.
ARRAS	11/6		2 Trucks arrived with Horse Shoes & Quilting & Pels &c	D.A.D.O.S. 3rd DIV^N
ARRAS	19/6		1 Truck Clothing arrived. 7 Tons Clothing & Saddlery	D.A.D.O.S. 3rd DIV^N
ARRAS	19/6		No Stores Arrived Stores Renewing Hot Clothing &c to Railhead	D.A.D.O.S. 3rd DIV^N
ARRAS	19/6		1 Truck Stores arrived (General Stores)	D.A.D.O.S. 3rd DIV^N
ARRAS LE-CAUROY	20/6		Moved to LE-CAUROY. 1 Truck Clothing arrived. Also 3 Vehicles (1 Mess Cart for H/A/H Y.D. 1 Wagon GS for 1C^o 3/D.T. & 1 K.T.Body for H/A Insⁿ)	D.A.D.O.S. 3rd DIVISION.
LE-CAUROY	21/6		No Trucks arrived. Lorries delivering Stores to 29th Div. Art. at ARRAS & drawing Stores from Gun Park.	D.A.D.O.S. 3rd DIVISION.

Army Form C.2118.

WAR DIARY
or
INTELLIGENCE SUMMARY.

(Erase heading not required.)

Instructions regarding War Diaries and Intelligence Summaries are contained in F.S. Regs., Part II. and the Staff Manual respectively. Title pages will be prepared in manuscript.

Place	Date	Hour	Summary of Events and Information	Remarks and references to Appendices
LE CAUROY	22/6/17		1 Truck Bits &c Arrived 9 1 Wagon Limbered G.S. for 20/1 K.R.R. delivering Stores to 3/Div. Art. at Wavrans 1 Lorry delivering Stores to 96-1 Bgde	D.A.D.O.S., 3rd DIVISION.
LE CAUROY	23/6/17		1 Truck Clothing Arrived	D.A.D.O.S., 3rd DIVISION.
LE CAUROY	24/6/17		1 Truck Horse Shoes Arrived 1 Lorry delivering Stores to 12/Div. for 29th Div. Art. Vet. 1 Lorry delivering Stores to 76-1 B.	D.A.D.O.S., 3rd DIVISION.
LE CAUROY	25/6/17		1 Truck Picketing Gear 9 36 Wheels Arrived. 2 Lorries delivering Stores to 3/Div. R.A. 9 1 Lorry drawing Gun parts &c from Gun Park.	D.A.D.O.S., 3rd DIVISION.
LE CAUROY	26/6/17		No Truck Arrived Lorries delivering Stores to R.O. 3/Div 9 96-1 I.B. 1 Lorry D. Clothing &c to Railhead.	D.A.D.O.S., 3rd DIVISION.
LE CAUROY	27/6/17		1 Truck Clothing Arrived 1 Lorry drawing Stores from Gun Park.	D.A.D.O.S., 3rd DIVISION.

Army Form C. 2118.

WAR DIARY
or
INTELLIGENCE SUMMARY.
(Erase heading not required.)

Instructions regarding War Diaries and Intelligence Summaries are contained in F. S. Regs., Part II. and the Staff Manual respectively. Title pages will be prepared in manuscript.

Place	Date	Hour	Summary of Events and Information	Remarks and references to Appendices
LE-CAUROY	28/1/17		No Stores turned Lorries clearing U Clothing &c to Railhead	D.A.D.O.S., 3rd DIVISION.
LE-CAUROY	29/1/17		9 delivering Stores to N.= S. B. 1 Truck Detail Stores Arrived	D.A.D.O.S., 3rd DIVISION. D.A.D.O.S., 3rd DIVISION.
LE-CAUROY	30/1/17		No Stores Arrived	D.A.D.O.S., 3rd DIVISION.

A. Seek, Captain
D.A.D.O.S., 3rd DIVISION.

Vol 36

Captain D J Jack. D.D.

D.A.D.D.S
3rd Div.

War Diary from 1/7/17 to 31/7/17

D.A.G.

3rd Echelon
Base

Attached please find War Diary for period 1/7/17 to 31/7/17

1/8/17

A.A.Jack, Captain

D.A.D.O.S.,
3rd DIVISION.

WAR DIARY
or
INTELLIGENCE SUMMARY.
(Erase heading not required.)

Army Form C. 2118.

Place	Date	Hour	Summary of Events and Information	Remarks and references to Appendices
LE-CAUROY Froricourt	1/7/17		Moved Dump to Froricourt	D.A.D.O.S., 3rd DIVISION.
Froricourt	2/7/17		No Truck arrived	D.A.D.O.S., 3rd DIVISION.
Froricourt	3/7/17		1 Truck Stores arrived	3rd DIVISION.
Froricourt	4/7/17		1 Truck Clothing arrived	A.D.O.S., 3rd DIVISION.
Froricourt	6/7/17		1 Truck Oils &c Arrived 1 Lorry drawing Stores from Gun Park.	3rd DIVISION.
Froricourt	7/7/17		1 Truck Horse Shoes &c arrived	

Army Form C. 2118

WAR DIARY
or
INTELLIGENCE SUMMARY.

(Erase heading not required.)

Instructions regarding War Diaries and Intelligence Summaries are contained in F. S. Regs. Part II. and the Staff Manual respectively. Title pages will be prepared in manuscript.

Place	Date	Hour	Summary of Events and Information	Remarks and references to Appendices
Armcourt	7/7		1 Truck Clothing Arrived.	D.A.D.O.S. 3rd DIVISION
Armcourt	8/7		No Stores Arrived	D.A.D.O.S. 3rd DIVISION
Armcourt	9/7		1 Truck Gen¹ Stores Arrived 2 Lorries drawing Stores from Gun Park.	D.A.D.O.S. 3rd DIVISION
Armcourt	10/7		No Stores Arrived 1 Lorry to Bapaume to draw Stores	D.A.D.O.S. 3rd DIVISION
Armcourt	11/7		1 Truck Clothing Arrived	D.A.D.O.S. 3rd DIVISION
Armcourt	12/7		1 Truck Soap Woollen Gds &c Arrived	A.D.O.S.

Army Form C. 2118.

WAR DIARY
or
INTELLIGENCE SUMMARY.
(Erase heading not required.)

Instructions regarding War Diaries and Intelligence Summaries are contained in F. S. Regs., Part II. and the Staff Manual respectively. Title pages will be prepared in manuscript.

Place	Date	Hour	Summary of Events and Information	Remarks and references to Appendices
Harmecourt	13/7/17		1 Truck Shoes Horse Arrived	D.A.D.O.S. 3rd DIVISION
Harmecourt	14/7/17		1 Truck Clothing Arrived	D.A.D.O.S. 3rd DIVISION
Harmecourt	15/7/17		1 Truck General Stores Arrived including 40 Wheels. 1 Kitchen Travelling Body for 10) King's 1 Water Cart & 1 Wagon G.S. for 2 Sets 3/0.C.	D.A.D.O.S. 3rd DIVISION
Harmecourt	16/7/17		No Stores Arrived	D.A.D.O.S. 3rd DIVISION
Harmecourt	17/7/17		1 Truck Gen. Stores Arrived & 1 Wagon G.S. for 129/R.F.A.	D.A.D.O.S. 3rd DIVISION

Army Form C. 2118.

WAR DIARY
or
INTELLIGENCE SUMMARY.
(Erase heading not required.)

Instructions regarding War Diaries and Intelligence Summaries are contained in F. S. Regs., Part II. and the Staff Manual respectively. Title pages will be prepared in manuscript.

Place	Date	Hour	Summary of Events and Information	Remarks and references to Appendices
Franicourt	18/7		1 Truck Clothing Arrived. 1 Lorry drawing Tents from H & Corps Troops for 9th Brigade	D.A.D.O.S., 3rd DIVISION.
Franicourt	19/7		1 Truck Bits & Pants &c Arrived. 1 Lorry to Gun Park drawing Stores. R.E Limber arrived for 3) Sig. Co. R.E.	D.A.D.O.S., 3rd DIVISION.
Franicourt	20/7.		1 Truck Shoes Horse Arrived	D.A.D.O.S., 3rd DIVISION.
Franicourt	21/7		1 Truck Clothing Arrived	D.A.D.O.S., 3rd DIVISION.
Franicourt	22/7		1 Lorry Food Gun Part Stores Received from 9 A.F.O. 1 Wagon G.S. arrived for 2/R. Scots 1 Cart Water for 8 F Amb 3 H.a.2.F.A. Ches 9 C.o.R.F.	D.A.D.O.S.,

Army Form C. 2118.

WAR DIARY
or
INTELLIGENCE SUMMARY.
(Erase heading not required.)

Instructions regarding War Diaries and Intelligence Summaries are contained in F. S. Regs., Part II. and the Staff Manual respectively. Title pages will be prepared in manuscript.

Place	Date	Hour	Summary of Events and Information	Remarks and references to Appendices
Harmicourt	23/7/17		1 Truck Picketing Gear Arrived. 1 Limber AT 1st for 149 Bde AFA arrived 1 Lorry drawing Stores from Gun Park	D.A.D.O.S., 3rd DIVISION.
Harmicourt	24/7/17		1 Truck Gun Stores Arrived	D.A.D.O.S., 3rd DIVISION.
Harmicourt	25/7/17		1 Truck Clothing Arrived	D.A.D.O.S., 3rd DIVISION.
Harmicourt	26/7/17		1 Truck Paint Oil & Soap Arrived 1 Lorry drawing Stores from Gun Park.	D.A.D.O.S., 3rd DIVISION.
Harmicourt	27/7/17		1 Truck Horse Shoes Arrived	D.A.D.O.S., 3rd DIVISION.
Harmicourt	28/7/17		1 Truck Clothing Arrived	D.A.D.O.S., 3rd DIVISION.

Army Form C. 2118.

WAR DIARY
or
INTELLIGENCE SUMMARY.
(Erase heading not required.)

Instructions regarding War Diaries and Intelligence Summaries are contained in F. S. Regs., Part II. and the Staff Manual respectively. Title pages will be prepared in manuscript.

Place	Date	Hour	Summary of Events and Information	Remarks and references to Appendices
Frevincourt	29/7		No Stores Arrived	D.A.D.O.S., 3rd DIVISION.
Frevincourt	30/7		1 Truck Gun Stores Arrived. 1 Lorry drawing Stores from Gun Park.	D.A.D.O.S., 3rd DIVISION.
Frevincourt	31/7		No Stores Arrived	D.A.D.O.S., 3rd DIVISION.

N. Jack. Captain.

D.A.D.O.S., 3rd DIVISION.

3   ⟨SECRET⟩

The D.A.G.
Kasi.

Herewith War Diary
for month of August 1917.

31/8/17   J.J.Jack. Captain
                   [D.A.D.O.S., 3rd DIVISION.]

WAR DIARY
or
INTELLIGENCE SUMMARY.

(Erase heading not required.)

Army Form C. 2118.

DADOS 3 Div Vol 37

Place	Date	Hour	Summary of Events and Information	Remarks and references to Appendices
Framecourt	1/8/17		1 Truck Stores Arrived	D.A.D.O.S., 3rd DIVISION.
Framecourt	2/8/17		No Stores Arrived at Railhead. 1 Lorry drawing Stores from Gun Park.	D.A.D.O.S., 3rd DIVISION.
Framecourt	3/8/17		No Stores Arrived. 4 Forges drawing Tentage for Div. H.Q.	D.A.D.O.S., 3rd DIVISION.
Framecourt	4/8/17		2 Trucks Clothing, Oil Soup, Horseshoes &c Arrived	D.A.D.O.S., 3rd DIVISION.
Framecourt	5/8/17		No Stores Arrived.	D.A.D.O.S., 3rd DIVISION.
Framecourt	6/8/17		No Stores Arrived	D.A.D.O.S., 3rd DIVISION.

Army Form C. 2118.

WAR DIARY
or
INTELLIGENCE SUMMARY.
(Erase heading not required.)

Instructions regarding War Diaries and Intelligence Summaries are contained in F. S. Regs., Part II. and the Staff Manual respectively. Title pages will be prepared in manuscript.

Place	Date	Hour	Summary of Events and Information	Remarks and references to Appendices
Frémicourt	7/8		2 Truck of Stores arrived. 1 Lorry drawing Stores from Gun Park.	D.A.D.O.S., 3rd DIVISION.
Frémicourt	8/8		1 Truck Stores arrived.	D.A.D.O.S., 3rd DIVISION.
Frémicourt	9/8		No Stores arrived. Lorry drawing 19 Gas Cylinders from IV Corps Corps.	D.A.D.O.S., 3rd DIVISION.
Frémicourt	11/8		2 Trucks Stores arrived.	3rd DIVISION
Frémicourt	11/8		2 Truck Stores arrived (1 containing 3 Mess Carts - 1 for each Field Coy R.E.). 1 Lorry drawing Stores from Gun Park.	3rd DIVISION
Frémicourt	12/8		1 Truck Stores arrived. (20 Bicycles - to substitute Horses). 16 Stretcher Horses drawn from II Corps Corps.	D.A.D.O.S. 3rd DIVISION

2353 Wt. W2544/1451 700,000 5/15 D. D. & L. A.D.S.S. Forms/C 2118.

Army Form C. 2118.

WAR DIARY
or
INTELLIGENCE SUMMARY.
(Erase heading not required.)

Instructions regarding War Diaries and Intelligence Summaries are contained in F. S. Regs., Part II. and the Staff Manual respectively. Title pages will be prepared in manuscript.

Place	Date	Hour	Summary of Events and Information	Remarks and references to Appendices
Ennemain	13/8/17		No stores arrived. (500 Rattles for men during Gas Shell attacks received.)	D.A.D.O.S., 3rd DIVISION
Ennemain	14/8/17		No Stores arrived.	D.A.D.O.S., 3rd DIVISION
Ennemain	15/8/17		2 Trucks Stores arrived. 1 Bivouac Hut received from C.T.E.	D.A.D.O.S., 3rd DIVISION
Ennemain	16/8/17		2 Trucks stores arrived. Lorry drawing Stores from Gun Park.	D.A.D.O.S., 3rd DIVISION
Ennemain	17/8/17		1 Truck Stores Arrived.	D.A.D.O.S., 3rd DIVISION
Ennemain	18/8/17		1 Truck Stores arrived.	D.A.D.O.S., 3rd DIVISION

Army Form C. 2118.

WAR DIARY
or
INTELLIGENCE SUMMARY.
(Erase heading not required.)

Instructions regarding War Diaries and Intelligence Summaries are contained in F. S. Regs., Part II. and the Staff Manual respectively. Title pages will be prepared in manuscript.

Place	Date	Hour	Summary of Events and Information	Remarks and references to Appendices
Frémicourt	19/5/17		1 Truck Stores Arrived.	3rd D.V.O.N. D.A.D.O.S. 3rd Div—
Frémicourt	20/5/17		No Stores arrived 1 Lorry drawing Stores from Gun Park.	
Frémicourt	21/5/17		1 Truck Stores arrived	
Frémicourt	22/5/17		1 Truck Stores arrived 1 Lorry drawing Stores from Gun Park.	3rd D.V.O.N.
Frémicourt	23/5/17		2 Stores arrived. 1 Lorry drawing mornings from Heavy Mobile Workshop.	3rd D.V.O.N.
Frémicourt	24/5/17		2 Trucks Stores arrived	D.A.D.O.S. 3rd Div—
Frémicourt	25/5/17		1 Truck Stores Arrived. Lorry drawing Stores from Gun Park.	D.A.D.O.S. 3rd D.V.O.N.

Army Form C. 2118.

WAR DIARY
or
INTELLIGENCE SUMMARY.
(Erase heading not required.)

Instructions regarding War Diaries and Intelligence Summaries are contained in F. S. Regs., Part II. and the Staff Manual respectively. Title pages will be prepared in manuscript.

Place	Date	Hour	Summary of Events and Information	Remarks and References to Appendices
Fremicourt	26/8/17		1 Truck Stores arrived.	
Fremicourt	27/8/17		1 Truck Stores arrived	
Fremicourt	28/8/17		No Stores arrived.	
Fremicourt	29/8/17		1 Truck Stores arrived. 1 Lorry Range Sheba from P. and B.T. Depot.	
Fremicourt	30/8/17		2 Trucks Stores arrived 1 Lorry drawing Stores from Gun Park.	
Fremicourt	31/8/17		1 Truck Stores arrived	

2353 Wt W2544/1454 700,000 5/15 D. D. & L. A.D.S.S.Forms/C. 2118.

4   Secret

D.A.G
3rd Echelon

Attached please find
A.&C/2118 (War Diary) for
month of September 1917.

A.J.Jack. Captain

D. A. D. O. S.
3rd Division
1 OCT. 1917

WAR DIARY
or
INTELLIGENCE SUMMARY.

DADOS 3 D Vol 38

Place	Date	Hour	Summary of Events and Information	Remarks and references to Appendices
Fremicourt	1/9/17		1 Truck Stores arrived. (5 tons Clothing)	D.A.D.O.S., 3rd DIVISION
Fremicourt	2/9/17		2 Trucks arrived (6 tons studs and General Stores). 1 Mac. Cart. for 4th Royal Fusiliers.	D.A.D.O.S., 3rd DIVISION
Fremicourt	3/9/17		1 Truck arrived with 1 Shoe Leather Limber and 1 Water Cart.	D.A.D.O.S., 3rd DIVISION
Bremicourt	4/9/17		1 Truck Stores Arrived. 1 Long taking Stores to 24th Division.	D.A.D.O.S., 3rd DIVISION
Fremicourt	5/9/17		1 Truck Clothing arrived and 513 Water Cans.	D.A.D.O.S., 3rd DIVISION
Fremicourt	6/9/17		2 Trucks Vehicles arrived. (1 Limbered Wagon 1 Bdy G.T. Cart 1 Limber AF 4.5" Hos(zier))	D.A.D.O.S., 3rd DIVISION
Ragnigny	7/9/17		1 Truck arrived (Clothing, Oil, Grease and Paint).	D.A.D.O.S., 3rd DIVISION

Army Form C. 2118.

WAR DIARY
or
INTELLIGENCE SUMMARY.
(Erase heading not required.)

Place	Date	Hour	Summary of Events and Information	Remarks and references to Appendices
Rocquigny	8/9/17		1 Truck Clothing arrived and 1087 Rum Water.	D.A.D.O.S., 3rd DIVISION.
Rocquigny	9/9/17		1 Truck General Stores P.H. Debaile arrived.	D.A.D.O.S., 3rd DIVISION
Rocquigny	10/9/17		No Stores arrived.	
Rocquigny	11/9/17		1 Truck arrived. L/C Robins K.T. 1 Body Lumbras Wagon R. & Lorries and Lorry drivers attached left to join 16th Supply Column.	3rd DIVISION
Rocquigny	12/9/17		1 Truck Clothing arrived.	D.A.D.O.S., 3rd DIVISION
Rocquigny	13/9/17		1 Truck Stores Shoes and oil arrived. 1 Kitchen Travelling arrived for 8/R.D.R.L. 1 Lorry drawing Stores from Gun Park	D.A.D.O.S., 3rd DIVISION
Rocquigny	14/9/17		1 N.O. & 2 N.C.O.'s proceed to WATOU with 1 Lorry of Stores for 3/Div. Art. No Stores arrived	D.A.D.O.S., 3rd DIVISION

Army Form C. 2118.

WAR DIARY
or
INTELLIGENCE SUMMARY.
(Erase heading not required.)

Place	Date	Hour	Summary of Events and Information	Remarks and references to Appendices
Roeaminghem	16/9		No Stores Arrived	
Roeaminghem	16/9		No Stores Arrived	
Roeaminghem Waten	17/9		Office & Dump moved to Waten	
Waten	18/9		No Stores Arrived	
Waten	19/9		No Stores Arrived	
Waten	20/9		No Stores Arrived	

Army Form C. 2118.

WAR DIARY
or
INTELLIGENCE SUMMARY.
(Erase heading not required.)

Instructions regarding War Diaries and Intelligence Summaries are contained in F. S. Regs., Part II. and the Staff Manual respectively. Title pages will be prepared in manuscript.

Place	Date	Hour	Summary of Events and Information	Remarks and references to Appendices
HATOU	21/9		No Trucks Arrived. 2 - 3" Stokes Guns rec'd for 76/TMB from 6th A.G.P. 198 Sets Packsaddlery drawn from DVTC Troops. 9/100 segs from DADOS 9th Div.	D.A.D.O.S., 3rd DIVISION.
HATOU	22/9		No Stores arrived	A.D.O.S., 3rd DIVISION.
HATOU	23/9		2 TRUCKS General STORES arrived.	
HATOU / POPERINGHE	24/9		Office & Dump moved to Poperinghe. No Stores from Railhead. 2 Lorry loads of Stores rec'd from 9/Div for AH2 Artillery Units - " - " - 6th Army Gun Park	D.A.D.O.S., 3rd DIVISION.
POPERINGHE	25/9		No Stores from Railhead. 1 Lorry of Stores from 9/Div for att'd Artillery Units	A.D.O.S, 3rd DIVISION.
POPERINGHE	26/9		2 Trucks Clothing & General Stores arrived, also 1 Lorry of Stores received from Gun Park	D.A.D.O.S., 3rd DIVISION.

Army Form C. 2118.

WAR DIARY
or
INTELLIGENCE SUMMARY.
(Erase heading not required.)

Instructions regarding War Diaries and Intelligence Summaries are contained in F. S. Regs., Part II. and the Staff Manual respectively. Title pages will be prepared in manuscript.

Place	Date	Hour	Summary of Events and Information	Remarks and references to Appendices
Poperinghe	27/9		No Stores arrived. 1. Water Cart received for D. Bay	D.A.D.O.S., 3rd DIVISION. 38 S & D Ag.
Poperinghe	28/9		2 Trucks Horse Shoes & arrived. 1 Wagon G.S. for A.L. 69th R.F.A. 1 Lorry of Gun parts & received from Gun Park	D.A.D.O.S., 3rd DIVISION.
Poperinghe	29/9		No Stores arrived	A.D.O.S., 3rd DIVISION.
Poperinghe Winnezeele	30/9		2 Trucks General Stores arrived. Moved Office & Dump to Winnezeele	D.A.D.O.S., 3rd DIVISION.

A. Jack, Captain
D.A.D.O.S. 3/Div

1/10/17

D.A.Q
3/ Echelon

Attached please
find A.F.C. 2118 (War Diary)
for month of October 1917

A. S. Jack. Captain

D. A. D. O. S.
3rd Division
31 OCT. 1917

WAR DIARY or INTELLIGENCE SUMMARY

Army Form C. 2118.

DADOS 3D
Vol 39

Place	Date	Hour	Summary of Events and Information	Remarks and references to Appendices
Winnyzeele	1/10		No Stores arrived	
Winnyzeele	2/10		No Stores arrived	
Winnyzeele	3/10		2 H.D. "New" arrived & handed over to Fifth Army Gun Park. Fontage (2 Marquees) received from Rouen & small quantity of Gun Parts for Art. which were sent to 3/Aust. Div. to whom 3/Div Art. less regt. attached	
Winnyzeele / Renescure	4/10		Moved Office & Dump to Renescure.	
Renescure	5/10		No Stores arrived. Division on the move	
Renescure / Baraste	6/10		Moved Office & Dump to Baraste	
Baraste	7/10		No Stores arrived. 1 Lorry lt. to 3/Aust. Div. to draw Stores &c. for 3/Div. Art. att'd to 3/Aus. Div	

Army Form C. 2118.

WAR DIARY
or
INTELLIGENCE SUMMARY.
(Erase heading not required.)

Instructions regarding War Diaries and Intelligence
Summaries are contained in F. S. Regs., Part II.
and the Staff Manual respectively. Title pages
will be prepared in manuscript.

Place	Date	Hour	Summary of Events and Information	Remarks and references to Appendices
Banastre	8/10		No Stores Arrived	
Banastre	9/10		1 Lorry to THIRD ARMY GUN PARK to draw 24 Lewis Guns. No Stores arrived at Haithuet. 1 Lorry to 4 Corps Troops to draw Tents for 9th J.B.	
Banastre	10/10		No Stores arrived at Haithuet. 2 Lorries drawing Tent Bottoms from 11th C. Tps & 1 Lorry delivering Tents to 9th & 76th Bdes.	
Banastre	11/10		No Stores arrived at Haithuet	
Banastre Monchaux Soncamp	12/10		Moved Dump & Office to Monchaux Soncamp. 7 Tons Clothing, 2000 Horse Rugs & Detail Stores arrived. 1 Lorry to Gun Park drawing 4 Vickers Guns &	
Monchaux Soncamp	13/10		1 Truck Clothing & 3 Trucks Blankets Arrived. 2 Lorries drawing Gun Bags & Tent Bonds from 4th C.T.	

2353 Wt. W2544/1454 700,000 5/15 D. D. & L. A.D.S.S. Forms/C. 2118.

Army Form C. 2118.

WAR DIARY
or
INTELLIGENCE SUMMARY.
(Erase heading not required.)

Instructions regarding War Diaries and Intelligence Summaries are contained in F. S. Regs., Part II. and the Staff Manual respectively. Title pages will be prepared in manuscript.

Place	Date	Hour	Summary of Events and Information	Remarks and references to Appendices
Monument Commonalty	14/10		1 Truck Blankets, 2 Trucks Clothing & 1 Truck Gen. Stores arrived at Railhead. Also 5 Vehicles for units	D.A.D.O.S., 3rd DIVISION.
Monument Commonalty	15/10		G.S. Stores arrived at Railhead. 156 prs Gum Boots Thigh received from 62/Div.	D.A.D.O.S., 3rd DIVISION.
Monument Commonalty	16/10		1 Truck General Stores arrived. 1 Lorry drawing Stores from Gun Park	D.A.D.O.S., 3rd DIVISION.
Monument Commonalty	17/10		3 Trucks Clothing & Necessaries arrived. 330 prs Gum Boots Thigh received from 62/Div.	D.A.D.O.S., 3rd DIVISION.
Monument Commonalty	18/10		3 Trucks Blankets arrived	D.A.D.O.S., 3rd DIVISION.
Monument Commonalty	19/10		1 Truck Oils Dubbing & Horse Shoes & 6 Trucks Blankets to Comp: 2 per man.	D.A.D.O.S., 3rd DIVISION.

WAR DIARY
or
INTELLIGENCE SUMMARY.

(Erase heading not required.)

Army Form C. 2118.

Place	Date	Hour	Summary of Events and Information	Remarks and references to Appendices
Movement Commencement	20/10		1 Truck Clothing 2 Trucks Leather jerkins & Undercoats for Infy.	D.A.D.O.S., 3rd DIVISION.
Movement Commencement	21/10		No Stores arrived at Railhead	D.A.D.O.S., 3rd DIVISION.
Movement Commencement	22/10		1 Truck Gen: Stores arrived 2 Travelling Kitchen Horses (1 for M/NF) (1 for A/NF)	D.A.D.O.S., 3rd DIVISION.
Movement Commencement	23/10		1 Truck Gen: Stores, Stoves Serges, Paillasses &c 2 Motor Lois for 12th Yorks 1 Lorry drawing Stores from Gun Park 1 Lorry delivering Stores to Gun Park etc	D.A.D.O.S., 3rd DIVISION.
Movement Commencement	24/10		1 Truck Gen: Stores 1 1 Truck Winter Clothing arrived	D.A.D.O.S., 3rd DIVISION.
Movement Commencement	25/10		No Stores arrived at Railhead 1 Lorry drawing Stores from Gun Park	D.A.D.O.S., 3rd DIVISION.

Army Form C. 2118.

WAR DIARY
or
INTELLIGENCE SUMMARY.
(Erase heading not required.)

Instructions regarding War Diaries and Intelligence Summaries are contained in F. S. Regs., Part II. and the Staff Manual respectively. Title pages will be prepared in manuscript.

Place	Date	Hour	Summary of Events and Information	Remarks and references to Appendices
Movement Commencealp	26/10		2 Trucks arrived, containing 400 Braziers, Grease, oil, Soap & Horse Shoes.	D.A.D.O.S. 3rd Division 26 OCT 1917
Movement Commencealp	27/10		2 Trucks Arrived Containing Clothing S.D. & Winter Clothing, also 400 Ins Waterslings. 1 Lorry delivering Packsaddling to 2D It Corps Troops.	D.A.D.O.S. 3rd DIVISION
Movement Commencealp	28/10		No Stores Arrived at Railhead. 4 Lorries drawing 50 Sets Tent Bottoms from N.C.T.S.	D.A.D.O.S. 3rd DIVISION
Movement Commencealp	29/10		No Stores Arrived at Railhead. 2 Lorries drawing 6 T.M.s from W.C. Troops. 1 Lorry -"- Stores from Gun Park.	D.A.D.O.S. 3rd DIVISION
Movement Commencealp	30/10		1 Truck General Stores Arrived. 2 Lorries delivery Stores to Area Comd & 1 Lorry drawing Stores from NCTS & drawing Tent Bottoms	D.A.D.O.S. 3rd DIVISION
Movement Commencealp	31/10		1 Truck General Stores Arrived	D.A.D.O.S. 3rd Division 31 OCT 1917

D.A.G.
3rd Echelon

Secret

Attached please find A.F.C. 2118 (War Diary) for month of November 1917.

30/11/17.

A.S.Jack. Captain

D.A.D.O.S.,
3rd DIVISION.

Army Form C. 2118.

WAR DIARY
or
INTELLIGENCE SUMMARY. DADOS 3/DIV.
(Erase heading not required.)

Vol 4

Place	Date	Hour	Summary of Events and Information	Remarks and references to Appendices
Divisional Commissariat	1/11		3 Trucks Gen. Stores arrived	
Divisional Commissariat	2/11		1 Truck Horse Shoes Arrived 1 Lorry drawing Stores from Gun Park	
Divisional Commissariat	3/11		2 Trucks Clothing Arrived at Railhead	
Divisional Commissariat	4/11		1 Truck General Stores Arrived	
Divisional Commissariat	5/11		1 Truck General Stores Arrived	
Divisional Commissariat	6/11		1 Truck Detail Stores Arrived, Also 1 Water Cart for your DAC & 1 Kit Bag for Gmore	

WAR DIARY
or
INTELLIGENCE SUMMARY.

(Erase heading not required.)

Army Form C. 2118.

Place	Date	Hour	Summary of Events and Information	Remarks and references to appendices
Havrincourt Communeship	4/11		1 Truck Clothing arrived, also 2 Travelling Kitchens for 8/By RFA 4 Lorries drawing Tents & Tent Bottoms for D.I.C requirements	D.A.D.O.S, 3rd DIVISION
Havrincourt Communeship	5/11		No Stores Arrived	D.A.D.O.S, 3rd DIVISION
Havrincourt Communeship	6/11		1 Truck General Stores arrived, also 1000 Blankets to complete issue of 3 per man.	D.A.D.O.S, 3rd DIVISION
Havrincourt Communeship	10/11		3½ Tons Clothing arrived in Truck with 51/Div. Stores	D.A.D.O.S, 3rd DIVISION
Havrincourt Communeship	11/11		No Stores Arrived	D.A.D.O.S, 3rd DIVISION
Havrincourt Communeship	12/11		1 Truck Gen. Stores arrived, also 1 Cart-hand common for Sig. Sub Sect. A of By 149th 149th F.A. & 1 Limbered Wagon for 3/Sect. 3/D.A.C	D.A.D.O.S, 3rd DIVISION

Army Form C. 2118.

WAR DIARY
or
INTELLIGENCE SUMMARY.
(Erase heading not required.)

Instructions regarding War Diaries and Intelligence Summaries are contained in F. S. Regs., Part II. and the Staff Manual respectively. Title pages will be prepared in manuscript.

Place	Date	Hour	Summary of Events and Information	Remarks and references to Appendices
Monument Commencourt	13/11		No Stores Arrived 1 Lorry drawing packsaddling for MCT's & 1 Lorry delivering Stores to Gun Carrs.	D.A.D.O.S. 3rd Division 14 NOV 1917
Monument Commencourt	14/11		2 Trucks Clothing & General Stores received. Also 1 3" TM for 9/TMB	D.A.D.O.S. 3rd DIVISION
Monument Commencourt	15/11		1 GS Wagon arrived for 9 Sect. 3) DAC 2 H.S." Hav't & Carriages arrived 1 for 29? 1 for 130? Bde. R.F.A.	D.A.D.O.S. 3rd DIVISION
Monument Commencourt	16/11		1 Truck Horse Shoes Clothing &c Arrived 1 Lorry drawing Stores from Gun Park	D.A.D.O.S. 3rd DIVISION
Monument Commencourt	17/11		1 Truck Clothing arrived 4 - 2" T.M^s arrived 2 Lorries drawing 100 Gun Axes from MCT's Stores from Gun Park	D.A.D.O.S. 3rd DIVISION
Monument Commencourt	18/11		No Stores Arrived.	D.A.D.O.S. 3rd DIVISION

Army Form C. 2118.

WAR DIARY
or
INTELLIGENCE SUMMARY.
(Erase heading not required.)

Instructions regarding War Diaries and Intelligence Summaries are contained in F. S. Regs., Part II. and the Staff Manual respectively. Title pages will be prepared in manuscript.

Place	Date	Hour	Summary of Events and Information	Remarks and references to Appendices
Monument Commencourt	19/11		No Stores Arrived	D.A.D.O.S., 3rd DIVISION. No. Date.
Monument Commencourt	20/11		No Stores Arrived	D.A.D.O.S., 3rd DIVISION. No. Date.
Monument Commencourt	21/11		3 Trucks Arrived Clothing, General Stores & reconsigned Stores for 20/K.R.R.	D.A.D.O.S., 3rd DIVISION. No. Date.
Monument Commencourt	22/11		1 Cart water for 130 Bde R.F.A. & 1 Bdy Kitchen Travelling Arrived for 20/K.R.R.	D.A.D.O.S., 3rd DIVISION. No. Date.
Monument Commencourt	23/11		1 Truck Horse Shoes & Dubbing Arrived	D.A.D.O.S., 3rd DIVISION. No. Date.
Monument Commencourt	24/11		1 Truck Clothing. Also reconsigned Stores from 63/DIV. for 20/K.R.R.	D.A.D.O.S., 3rd DIVISION. No. Date.

Army Form C. 2118.

WAR DIARY
or
INTELLIGENCE SUMMARY.
(Erase heading not required.)

Instructions regarding War Diaries and Intelligence Summaries are contained in F. S. Regs., Part II. and the Staff Manual respectively. Title pages will be prepared in manuscript.

Place	Date	Hour	Summary of Events and Information	Remarks and references to Appendices
Monument Commencerup	26/11		No Stores arrived at Railhead	D.A.D.O.S. 3rd DIVISION [stamp/signature]
Monument Commencerup	27/11		No Stores arrived at Railhead	D.A.D.O.S. 3rd DIVISION [stamp/signature]
Monument Commencerup	28/11		1 Truck General Stores arrived	D.A.D.O.S. 3rd DIVISION [stamp/signature]
Monument Commencerup	28/11		1 Truck Clothing arrived.	D.A.D.O.S. 3rd DIVISION [stamp/signature]
Monument Commencerup	29/11		1 Truck Pet Oc arrived, also 2, 3" Stokes guns for 4/TMB.	D.A.D.O.S. 3rd DIVISION [stamp/signature]
Monument Commencerup	30/11		1 Truck Horse Shoes arrived	D.A.D.O.S. 3rd DIVISION [stamp/signature]

[signature] Captain
DADOS 3/DIV.

D.A.G
3rd Echelon

Attached please find A.F.C. 2118 (War Diary) for month of December 1917

"Deane Cond"
for

D. A. D. O. S.
3rd Division
31 DEC 1917

WAR DIARY

INTELLIGENCE SUMMARY

Army Form C. 2118.

DADOS 3/DIV.

Place	Date	Hour	Summary of Events and Information	Remarks and references to Appendices
Monchaux Commencourt	1/12/17		3 Tons Clothing Arrived	
Monchaux Commencourt	2/12/17		Whgls & Gun Parts received from Calais Also 1, 3" T.M. for 9th T.M.B.	
Monchaux Commencourt	3/12/17		1 Truck General Stores Arrived. 6 A.A. L.G. M.gs recd from 3/AT.Nº1.	
Monchaux Commencourt	4/12/17		No Stores Arrived	
Monchaux Commencourt	5/12/17		4 Tons Clothing Arrived.	
Monchaux Commencourt	6/12/17		8 Tons General Stores arrived Also 1 Body M.T. for 13/King's 2 Wagons Limbered for 3/Sec D.A.C. & 1 Wagn Limbered for 2/R. Scots.	

Army Form C. 2118.

WAR DIARY
or
INTELLIGENCE SUMMARY.

(Erase heading not required.)

2nd Sheet

Instructions regarding War Diaries and Intelligence Summaries are contained in F. S. Regs., Part II. and the Staff Manual respectively. Title pages will be prepared in manuscript.

Place	Date	Hour	Summary of Events and Information	Remarks and references to Appendices
Advanced Remount Commissariat	4/12		1 Truck General Stores arrived. 4 Chaff Cutters returned to 3rd D.A.C.	A.D.O.S., 3rd DIVISION.
Advanced Remount Commissariat	5/12		1 Truck Clothing Arrived. 2. 4.5" How" drawn from G.P.s & handed over to 5 D.M. 1 Vickers Gun drawn from G.S. for 2/Ch G.C.	D.A.D.O.S., 3rd DIVISION.
Advanced Remount Commissariat	6/12		1 Truck Horse Shoes &c. Arrived	D.A.D.O.S., 3rd DIVISION.
Advanced Remount Commissariat	7/12		1 Truck Vehicles Arrived. 1 Motor Cart Cash for Hqrs Batt. A.F.A. 2 New D.A.C. & 87E Yorks. 1 Wagon limbered G.S. each for 8/E Yorks & 2/11 Scotn.	A.D.O.S., 3rd DIVISION.
Advanced Remount Commissariat	8/12		Oil Stores Arrived at Railhead. 3 T.M Barrels 3" Arrived for 8/T.M.B.	A.D.O.S., 3rd DIVISION.
Advanced Remount Commissariat	9/12		1 Truck Clothing Arrived, also 400 Tons Water. 4 Newsums recd for 104 F.A.	D.A.D.O.S., 3rd DIVISION.
Advanced Remount Commissariat	10/12		Oil Stores Arrived at Railhead	D.A.D.O.S., 3rd DIVISION.

Army Form C. 2118.

WAR DIARY
or
INTELLIGENCE SUMMARY.
(Erase heading not required.)

3rd Sheet

Instructions regarding War Diaries and Intelligence Summaries are contained in F. S. Regs., Part II. and the Staff Manual respectively. Title pages will be prepared in manuscript.

Place	Date	Hour	Summary of Events and Information	Remarks and references to Appendices
Monchaux Communicaux	14/12		3 Motor Carts Arrived for. 45th Pack MTC. 1/Gordons + 7/R.Scots 5 Lewis Guns rec'd (4 for 13/Kings Lpools - 1 for 2/Suffolks)	D.A.D.O.S., 3rd DIVISION
Monchaux Communicaux Graviliers	15/12		Cleared Office of Stores to Graviliers. 1 Truck Clothing Arrived. 2 Trucks General Stores Arrived	D.A.D.O.S., 3rd DIVISION
Graviliers	16/12		No Stores Arrived at Railhead. 1 Vickers Gun recd for L33/MGC. 2 Lewis Guns received for 8/KOR Lanc.	D.A.D.O.S., 3rd DIVISION
Graviliers	17/12		2 Motor Carts 1 Limbered Wagon 9. 1 Hind Portion Limbered Wagon. Arrived for 4/R.Fus. 25. 76/MGC & 13th Sqdn MGC. Lewis Guns received for 76/MGC & 13th Sqdn MGC.	D.A.D.O.S., 3rd DIVISION
Graviliers	18/12		9 Tons General Stores Arrived.	D.A.D.O.S., 3rd DIVISION
Graviliers	19/12		No Stores Arrived.	D.A.D.O.S., 3rd DIVISION

Army Form C. 2118.

H A Shea

WAR DIARY
or
INTELLIGENCE SUMMARY.
(Erase heading not required.)

Instructions regarding War Diaries and Intelligence Summaries are contained in F. S. Regs., Part II. and the Staff Manual respectively. Title pages will be prepared in manuscript.

Place	Date	Hour	Summary of Events and Information	Remarks and references to Appendices
ENNIKERS	20/12		No Stores arrived at Railhead	D.A.D.O.S. 3rd DIVISION.
ENNIKERS	21/12		4 Tons Clothing arrived at Railhead	D.A.D.O.S. 3rd DIVISION.
ENNIKERS	22/12		2 Trucks Gen. Stores Clothing, &c. Horseshoes &c Arrived at Railhead. 1 Wagon G.S. for 10/11 N.F. & 12/11 Yorks. 1 Wagon (incl^d G.S. Ammⁿ for 20/K.R.R. 2/ Rivers Sons (1 for 11 N.F. & 1 for 12 n. Yorks) rec^d from Adv^d. G.P.	D.A.D.O.S. 3rd DIVISION.
ENNIKERS	23/12		No Stores arrived at Railhead	D.A.D.O.S. 3rd DIVISION.
Enneller	24/12		No Stores arrived at Railhead	D.A.D.O.S. 3rd DIVISION.
Enneller	25/12		1 Truck Gen. Stores Arrived. THAW precautions in force and no lorries allowed on roads. 4 G.S. Wagons obtained from Town to Carry Stores	D.A.D.O.S. 3rd DIVISION.
Enneller	26/12		4 Tons Clothing received. THAW precautions Removed at 12 noon.	D.A.D.O.S. 3rd DIVISION.

Army Form C. 2118.

5th Sheet

WAR DIARY
or
INTELLIGENCE SUMMARY.
(Erase heading not required.)

Instructions regarding War Diaries and Intelligence Summaries are contained in F. S. Regs., Part II. and the Staff Manual respectively. Title pages will be prepared in manuscript.

Place	Date	Hour	Summary of Events and Information	Remarks and references to Appendices
Crevillers	27/12		No Stores arrived at Railhead	D.A.D.O.S. 3rd DIVISION
Crevillers	28/12		1 Truck Horse Shoes & General Stores arrived also 1 Water Cart for 12th R. Yorks & 1 Webby Travelling for 9th R Scots / Stores Sent out for 9th I. Bgde	D.A.D.O.S. 3rd DIVISION
Crevillers	29/12		1 Truck Clothing arrived / 1 Lorry drawing Stores from Gun Park	D.A.D.O.S. 3rd DIVISION
Crevillers	30/12		No Stores arrived at Railhead	D.A.D.O.S. 3rd DIVISION
Crevillers	31/12		No Stores arrived at Railhead	D.A.D.O.S. 3rd DIVISION

D.A.D.O.S.
3rd Division
31 DEC. 1917

WAR DIARY
or
INTELLIGENCE SUMMARY.

Army Form C. 2118

Place	Date	Hour	Summary of Events and Information	Remarks and references to Appendices
Givillers	1/1/16		No Stores arrived at Railhead	D.A.D.O.S. 3rd DIVISION
Givillers	2/1/15		1 Truck Clothing arrived at Railhead. 1 Lorry delivering Stores to 4th Div	D.A.D.O.S. 3rd DIVISION
Givillers	3/1/16		1 Truck General Stores arrived at Railhead 1 Lorry delivering stores to 9/1/13	D.A.D.O.S. 3rd DIVISION
Pondlers	4/1/16		1 Truck Horse Shoes arrived 1 Lorry delivering Stores to 10/1/13	D.A.D.O.S. 3rd DIVISION
Givillers	5/1/16		1 Truck Clothing arrived. 1 Lorry delivering Stores to 9/1/13	D.A.D.O.S. 3rd DIVISION
Pondlers	6/1/16		No Stores arrived at Railhead. 1 Lorry delivering Stores to 10/1/13	D.A.D.O.S. 3rd DIVISION

Army Form C. 2118.

WAR DIARY
or
INTELLIGENCE SUMMARY.
(Erase heading not required.)

Instructions regarding War Diaries and Intelligence Summaries are contained in F. S. Regs., Part II. and the Staff Manual respectively. Title pages will be prepared in manuscript.

Place	Date	Hour	Summary of Events and Information	Remarks and references to Appendices
Crotoys	7/1/16		1 Truck General Stores arrived 5 NCO's & men sent to Railhead to deal with stores for 9th & 76th Bde during thaw precautions	D.A.D.O.S. 3rd DIVISION
Crotoys	8/1/16		1 Wagon Ammⁿ Limber arrived for 29 Divn R.F.A.	D.A.D.O.S. 3rd DIVISION
Crotoys	9/1/16		1 Truck Clothing arrived at Railhead. 1 Kitchen Body arrived for 1 of T. 1 Motor cart for 3 Sig Co R.E. 1 Motor Part & 1 Wagon Limber & 1 Hind Part for 4 R.S.T.	D.A.D.O.S. 3rd DIVISION
Crotoys	10/1		1 Truck General Stores Arrived at Railhead	D.A.D.O.S. 3rd DIVISION
Crotoys	11/1		1 Truck Horse Shoes &c Arrived at Railhead	D.A.D.O.S. 3rd DIVISION
Crotoys	12/1		1 Truck Clothing arrived at Railhead. THAW precautions in force. 9 no lorries allowed on roads. H.G.S. Wagons obtained from 3 D.T. to bring stores from Railhead.	D.A.D.O.S. 3rd DIVISION

Army Form C. 2118.

WAR DIARY
or
INTELLIGENCE SUMMARY.
(Erase heading not required.)

Instructions regarding War Diaries and Intelligence Summaries are contained in F. S. Regs., Part II. and the Staff Manual respectively. Title pages will be prepared in manuscript.

Place	Date	Hour	Summary of Events and Information	Remarks and references to Appendices.
Erillers	13/1		No Stores arrived at Railhead	D.A.D.O.S. 3rd DIVISION.
Erillers	14/1		4 3" Stokes Mortars rec'd from Calais for 9/TMB-3. 8/TMB-1	D.A.D.O.S. 3rd DIVISION.
Erillers	15/1		1 Truck General Stores arrived at Railhead	D.A.D.O.S. 3rd DIVISION.
Erillers	16/1		1 Truck Clothing arrived at Railhead	D.A.D.O.S. 3rd DIVISION.
Erillers	17/1		No Stores arrived at Railhead	D.A.D.O.S. 3rd DIVISION.
Erillers	18/1		No Stores arrived at Railhead	D.A.D.O.S. 3rd DIVISION.
Erillers	19/1		1 Truck General Stores & 1 Truck Clothing arrived at Railhead	D.A.D.O.S. 3rd DIVISION.

Army Form C. 2118.

WAR DIARY
or
INTELLIGENCE SUMMARY.
(Erase heading not required.)

Instructions regarding War Diaries and Intelligence Summaries are contained in F. S. Regs., Part II. and the Staff Manual respectively. Title pages will be prepared in manuscript.

Place	Date	Hour	Summary of Events and Information	Remarks and references to Appendices
Ervillers	20/1		1 Truck General Stores Arrived at Railhead 1 Carriage 4'6" for D/18 & 9.1 1st C.P. spare for A5/RFC drawn from Advanced G.P. also 3 Vickers guns for 233 chy C	D.A.D.O.S., 3rd DIVISION.
Ervillers	21/1		No Stores Arrived at Railhead 3 18P" pieces drawn from Advanced Gun Park 2 for A/15 S+C & 1 for D/ 53+D	D.A.D.O.S., 3rd DIVISION.
Ervillers	22/1		1 Truck Stores Arrived at Railhead. THAW precautions removed from Midnight 21/22.1.18	D.A.D.O.S., 3rd DIVISION.
Ervillers	23/1		1 Truck Clothing Arrived at Railhead.	D.A.D.O.S., 3rd DIVISION.
Ervillers	24/1		No Stores Arrived at Railhead	D.A.D.O.S., 3rd DIVISION.
Ervillers	25/1		1 Truck General Stores Arrived at Railhead.	D.A.D.O.S., 3rd DIVISION.

Army Form C. 2118.

WAR DIARY
or
INTELLIGENCE SUMMARY.
(Erase heading not required.)

Place	Date	Hour	Summary of Events and Information	Remarks and references to Appendices
Erulles	26/1/18		2 Trucks Clothing & Gum Boots Thigh received at Railhead	D.A.D.O.S. 3rd DIVISION
Erulles	27/1/18		No Stores arrived at Railhead. Lorries moving Salvage to A'head	D.A.D.O.S. 3rd DIVISION
Erulles	28/1/18		No Stores arrived at Railhead.	D.A.D.O.S. 3rd DIVISION
Boulent sur front	29/1		2 Trucks Picketing Pegs and Shells received arrived. Truck Bomps and offered to Frehen-sur-front.	D.A.D.O.S. 3rd DIVISION D.A.D.S. 3rd DIVISION
Boulent sur front	30/1		1 Truck arrived with Long Clothing Boots Gum Child Erks etc at office. D.A.D.O.S. attended conference of A.D.O.S. VI Corps.	D.A.D.O.S. 3rd DIVISION
Boulent sur front	31/1		No Stores arrived at Railhead.	D.A.D.O.S. 3rd DIVISION

D.A.D.O.S.
3rd Division
31 JAN 1918

A. Jack Capt.

D.A.G.
3rd Echelon

Attached please find A.F.C. 2118 (War Diary) for month of February 1918.

D.S. Jack, Captain

D.A.D.O.S.
3rd Division
27 FEB. 1918

H Sheet 5

• D.A.D.O.S. 3rd DIVISION

Army Form C. 2118.

WAR DIARY
or
INTELLIGENCE SUMMARY.
(Erase heading not required.)

Vol 4 3

Place	Date	Hour	Summary of Events and Information	Remarks and references to Appendices
Boulou au Front	Feb 1st		No stores arrived at Railhead.	D.A.D.O.S. 3rd Division 1-FEB.1918
Boulou au Front	2nd		1 Truck Clothing arrived (Jackets, Trousers, Shorts, Puttees etc) Lorry drawing from and taking from XI Corps Coys.	D.A.D.O.S. 3rd Division 2-FEB.1918
Boulou au Front	3rd		2 Trucks arrived with Linens, Soap, Horseshoes etc. & Reshoeing up of 10th K.O.Y.L.I. Fatigue wagons Lumbers E.C.	D.A.D.O.S. 3rd Division 3-FEB.1918
Boulou au Front	4th		No stores arrived. 1 Lorry drawing Uniform Textile Coving	D.A.D.O.S. 3rd Division 4-FEB.1918
Boulou au Front	5th		No clothing arrived. Stores from 10th K.O.Y.L.I. Foresters being returned.	D.A.D.O.S. 3rd Division 5-FEB.1918
Boulou au Front	6th		1 Truck Clothing arrived Boots, Capes, Shirts, Socks, etc.	D.A.D.O.S. 3rd Division 6-FEB.1918
Boulou au Front	7th		1 Truck arrived with Trekking Gear Bot and Horse Respirators. Stores returned from 10th K.O.Y.L.I. despatched to Base Park.	D.A.D.O.S. 3rd Division 7-FEB.1918
Boulou au Front	8th		No stores arrived.	D.A.D.O.S. 3rd Division 8-FEB.1918

2nd Sheet

Army Form C. 2118.

WAR DIARY
or
INTELLIGENCE SUMMARY.
(Erase heading not required.)

Instructions regarding War Diaries and Intelligence Summaries are contained in F. S. Regs., Part II. and the Staff Manual respectively. Title pages will be prepared in manuscript.

Place	Date	Hour	Summary of Events and Information	Remarks and references to Appendices
Bienvillers au Bois	9th		1 Truck arrived (Nitride Hanover Stocks the) also 1 Sub. Park for V.3. T.M.B.	D.A.D.O.S. 3rd Division 10 FEB 1918
Bienvillers au Bois	10th		So Stores arrived. Lorry taking Stores to 4/2nd Rds. at SOUASTRE.	3rd Division 10 FEB 1918
Bienvillers au Bois	11th		10 Ton Stores arrived (Stores Chera - Port Sustaining gear). Breaking up 2 of 5th East Yorks - Lorry bringing Shrivel Stores from BOYELLES.	D.A.D.O.S. 3rd Division 11 FEB 1918
Bienvillers au Bois	12th		1 Truck containing 1 G.S. wagon 2 water Carts, 1 Spare Limber Limber and 1 Mess Cart arrived	D.A.D.O.S. 3rd Division 12 FEB 1918
Bienvillers au Bois	13th		No Stores arrived. Lorry taking Stores to Artillery at SOUASTRE.	D.A.D.O.S. 3rd Division 13 FEB 1918
Bienvillers au Bois	14th		2 Trucks arrived, Clothing, Group Respirators. 12th West Yorks being dis'tded - Stores being returned.	D.A.D.O.S. 3rd Div 14 FEB 1918
Berles au Bois	15th		No Stores arrived at Railhead. Lorry taking Stores to Artillery at SQUASTRE.	3rd Div 15 FEB 1918

Army Form C. 2118.

WAR DIARY
or
INTELLIGENCE SUMMARY.
(Erase heading not required.)

3rd Sheet

Instructions regarding War Diaries and Intelligence Summaries are contained in F. S. Regs., Part II. and the Staff Manual respectively. Title pages will be prepared in manuscript.

Place	Date	Hour	Summary of Events and Information	Remarks and references to Appendices
Boisleux-au-Mont	16th		1 Truck Clothing Arrived at Railhead. 1 Lorry drawing 4 6" How from Gun Park for D Batt. 19 S.J.O. Bgde. 4 Lewis Guns from D/H to yards S/6 yorks 9 H/H/H I handed over to Ordnance. G.P. Dispense.	D.A.D.O.S. 3rd Division 16 FEB 1918
Boisleux-au-Mont	17th		O/o Stores Arrived at Railhead. 1 Lorry delivering Stores to R.A. 2 Lorries drawing Tentage for Entrenching Battn.	D.A.D.O.S. 3rd Division 17 FEB 1918
Boisleux-au-Mont	18th		O/o Stores Arrived at Railhead. 1. 9+5 T.M. 9 8 & 2" T.M's withdrawn from Div. Art. vide THIRD ARMY C/1135. 9 taken to Railhead, for despatch as follows) 9+5 to Gun Park FIFTH ARMY. 9 2" T.M. to Base.	D.A.D.O.S. 3rd Division 18 FEB 1918
Boisleux-au-Mont	19th		30 Lewis guns rec'd from G.P. for issue to Inf 99 & Art for Anti Aircraft work. 1 Truck Stores Arrived from Havre.	D.A.D.O.S. 3rd Division 20 FEB 1918
Boisleux-au-Mont	20th		1 Truck Clothing Arrived at Railhead.	D.A.D.O.S. 3rd Division 20 FEB 1918
Boisleux-au-Mont	21st		O/o Stores Arrived at Railhead. 149 Sets Packsaddlery Returned to D.O.S/AT No 1.	D.A.D.O.S. 3rd Division 21 FEB 1918

4th Sheet

Army Form C. 2118.

WAR DIARY
or
INTELLIGENCE SUMMARY.
(Erase heading not required.)

Instructions regarding War Diaries and Intelligence Summaries are contained in F. S. Regs., Part II. and the Staff Manual respectively. Title pages will be prepared in manuscript.

Place	Date	Hour	Summary of Events and Information	Remarks and references to Appendices
Bustecu-au-mont	22nd		1 Truck Horse Shoes &c Arrived at Railhead.	22 FEB 1918 D.A.D.O.S.
Bustecu-au-mont	23rd		1 Truck Clothing Arrived at Railhead. 4 Lewis guns received for issue to R.E.Co's for Anti-Aircraft Defences.	23 FEB 1918 D.A.D.O.S.
Bustecu-au-mont	24th		No Stores Arrived at Railhead	24 FEB 1918 D.A.D.O.S.
Bustecu-au-mont	25th		No Stores Arrived at Railhead.	25 FEB 1918 D.A.D.O.S. 3rd Division
Bustecu-au-mont	26th		1 Truck General Stores Arrived at Railhead	26 FEB 1918 D.A.D.O.S. 3rd Division
Bustecu-au-mont	27th		1 Truck Clothing Arrived at Railhead	27 FEB 1918 D.A.D.O.S.
Bustecu-au-mont	28th		1 Truck Bedding &c &c Arrived at Railhead. 1 Coy of 24th M.R. detailed as fatigues & Stores being received from this Coy daily.	28 FEB 1918 D.A.D.O.S.

D. Jack, Captain
D.A.D.O.S.
3rd DIVISION

MEMORANDUM.

Army Form C 348 (Pads.)

From: D.A.D.O.S., 3rd DIVISION.
Date: 31 3 1918

To: DAG 3rd Echelon

Attached please find A.F.C 2118 (War Diary) for month of March 1918.

A.J.Jack. Captain

D.A.D.O.S.
3rd Division
31 MAR. 1918

Army Form C. 2118.

WAR DIARY
or
INTELLIGENCE SUMMARY.

(Erase heading not required.)

Instructions regarding War Diaries and Intelligence Summaries are contained in F. S. Regs., Part II. and the Staff Manual respectively. Title pages will be prepared in manuscript.

Place	Date	Hour	Summary of Events and Information	Remarks and references to Appendices
Bertius	1/3/18		No Stores Arrived at Railhead. 34 Lewis Guns recd. for Anti-Aircraft Defence	3rd Division 1 MAR 1918 D.A.D.O.S.
"	2/3/18		3½ Tons S.D. Clothing Arrived at Railhead	D.A.D.O.S. 3rd Division 2 MAR 1918
"	3/3/18		No Stores Arrived at Railhead	D.A.D.O.S. 3rd Division 3 MAR 1918
"	4/3/18		2 Trucks Gen. Stores Horse Shoes &c Arrived at Railhead	D.A.D.O.S. 3rd Division 5 MAR 1918
"	5/3/18		No Stores Arrived at Railhead. 1. 4.5" How: drawn from G.P. for 129 RFA.	D.A.D.O.S. 3rd Division 5 MAR 1918
"	6/3/18		1 Truck Clothing 1 Truck Gen Stores Arrived at Railhead. 1. 6 Pr Anti Tank gun recd. Issued to NCS 49. 5 Hotchkiss guns recd for L.G. Defence. Issued to D.T. 2WE & 10SCC.	D.A.D.O.S. 3rd Division 6 MAR 1918
"	7/3/18		No Stores Arrived at Railhead	D.A.D.O.S. 3rd Division 7 MAR 1918

Army Form C. 2118.

WAR DIARY
or
INTELLIGENCE SUMMARY.
(Erase heading not required.)

Instructions regarding War Diaries and Intelligence Summaries are contained in F. S. Regs., Part II. and the Staff Manual respectively. Title pages will be prepared in manuscript.

3rd Div.

Place	Date	Hour	Summary of Events and Information	Remarks and references to Appendices
Busteux-Wi- -prost	8/3/18		No Stores Arrived at Railhead	3rd Division 8 MAR 1918
Busteux-Wi- -prost	9/3/18		No Stores Arrived at Railhead. 1 Vickers M.G Drawn from G1 for 3/18th M.G.C.	D.A.D.O.S. 3rd Division 9 MAR 1918
"	10/3		1 Truck General Stores Arrived at Railhead	D.A.D.O.S. 3rd Division 10 MAR 1918
"	11/3		No Stores Arrived at Railhead	D.A.D.O.S. 3rd Division 11 MAR 1918
"	12/3		No Stores Arrived at Railhead	D.A.D.O.S. 3rd Division 12 MAR 1918
"	13/3		1 Truck Clothing & 1 Truck General Stores Arrived at Railhead	D.A.D.O.S. 3rd Division 13 MAR 1918
"	14/3		No Stores Arrived at Railhead	D.A.D.O.S. 3rd Division 14 MAR 1918
"	15/3		No Stores Arrived at Railhead	D.A.D.O.S. 3rd Division 15 MAR 1918

Army Form C. 2118.

WAR DIARY
or
INTELLIGENCE SUMMARY.
(Erase heading not required.)

Instructions regarding War Diaries and Intelligence Summaries are contained in F. S. Regs., Part II. and the Staff Manual respectively. Title pages will be prepared in manuscript.

Place	Date	Hour	Summary of Events and Information	Remarks and references to Appendices.
Bertrancourt	16/3		1 Truck General Stores & 1 Truck Clothing Arrived at Railhead	3rd Division 16 MAR 1918 D.A.D.O.S.
"	17/3		No Stores Arrived at Railhead today.	3rd Division 17 MAR 1918 D.A.D.O.S.
"	18/3		1 Truck Stores arrived at Railhead also 1 R.T. Body for 4/R.F. 1 Wagon Limbt R.B. for 4/38 Ches. & F.A. R.B.	3rd Division 18 MAR 1918 D.A.D.O.S.
"	19/3		No Stores Arrived at Railhead	3rd Division 19 MAR 1918 D.A.D.O.S.
"	20/3		No Stores Arrived at Railhead	3rd Division 20 MAR 1918 D.A.D.O.S.
"	21/3		1 Truck General Stores arrived at Railhead	3rd Division 21 MAR 1918 D.A.D.O.S.
Herrere	22/3		1 Truck General Stores Arrived at Railhead 1 G.S.L. & 1 R.T. Body for 2/R Scots D. Transport begins to Moved Office & Dump to Kirribre	3rd Division 22 MAR 1918 D.A.D.O.S.

Army Form C. 2118.

WAR DIARY
or
INTELLIGENCE SUMMARY.
(Erase heading not required.)

Place	Date	Hour	Summary of Events and Information	Remarks and references to Appendices
Hiren	23/3		1 Truck Clothing Arrived at Railhead. Also Clinical 3 Trucks Petbury for SDV&C Tps.	3rd Division 25 MAR 1918
	24/3		OM Stores Arrived at Railhead. 1 Lewis Guns drawn from G. Park for 4/18.R.K.R & 11/1.B & pet F. 1.15p & 1 Lewis Guns drawn from G. Park for 4/18.R.K.R & 11/1.B & pet F.	D.A.D.O.S. 3rd Division 24 MAR 1918
	25/3		OM Stores Arrived at Railhead. 4 Vickers Guns for 3/18"cd G C } Drawn from 9DV&CTps 1 Lewis — 4/1.B	D.A.D.O.S. 3rd Division 25 MAR 1918
	26/3		2 Trucks Arrived at Railhead. Boots & Hornette taken from Same 3" T.M.S -3 Arrived for 9/TM.B. 9 Armourer Returned to Base. Lorry Clearing Stores to Railhead for DV&CTps.	D.A.D.O.S. 3rd Division 26 MAR 1918
	27/3		10 Stores Arrived at Railhead. Lorry Clearing Stores to Railhead for DV&CTps.	D.A.D.O.S. 3rd Division 27 MAR 1918
Party	28/3		1 Truck Stores Arrived at Railhead. Vet Sub: Mm; 9 Mangoon, taken from Same to Barly. 9 Armourer Returned to Base. Clove Office & Dump to Barly.	D.A.D.O. 3rd Division 28 MAR 1918

Army Form C. 2118.

WAR DIARY
or
INTELLIGENCE SUMMARY.
(Erase heading not required.)

Instructions regarding War Diaries and Intelligence Summaries are contained in F. S. Regs., Part II. and the Staff Manual respectively. Title pages will be prepared in manuscript.

Place	Date	Hour	Summary of Events and Information	Remarks and references to Appendices
Party	29/3		No Stores Arrived at Railhead. Lorry Sent with Stores for Issue to 8th, 9th & 76th J Bgde.	D.A.D.O.S. 3rd Division 29 MAR 1918
"	30/3		No Stores Arrived at Railhead. 21 Lewis Guns Issued to 76th J B. Units.	D.A.D.O.S. 3rd Division 30 MAR 1918
"	31/3		1 Truck Vehicles Arrived at Railhead & Issued to Units. Transferred 242 Units to 1st Canadian DIV, 32 DIV & 90 3/ATDA	D.A.D.O.S. 3rd Division 31 MAR 1918

A.J. Jack, Captain

D.A.D.O.S. 3rd Division 31 MAR 1918

(4534). Wt. 8811—M 2754. 38 M Pads. 10-17. J. T. & S., Ltd. ~~Secret~~ Army Form C 348 (Pads.)

MEMORANDUM.

From: D.A.D.O.S. 3rd Division 30 APR. 1918

To: DAG 3rd Echelon

Date _____ 191

Attached please find A.F. C.2118 (War Diary) for Month of April 1918.

J. D. Jack, Captain

D.A.D.O.S. 3rd Division 30 APR. 1918

DADOS 3rd DIV

WAR DIARY

of

INTELLIGENCE SUMMARY.

(Erase heading not required.)

Army Form C. 2118.

Place	Date	Hour	Summary of Events and Information	Remarks and references to Appendices
BARLY	1/4		No Stores Arrived at Railhead. Moved Office & Dump to BRUAY.	D.A.D.O.S. 3rd Division 1 APR 1918
BRUAY	2/4		No Stores Arrived at Railhead.	D.A.D.O.S. 3rd Division 2 APR 1918
BRUAY	3/4		1 Truck Stores Arrived at Railhead. 1 Wagon Catts loaned for 3/Suff.? Moved Office & Dump to Fauquieres.	D.A.D.O.S. 3rd Division 3 APR 1918
Fauquieres	4/4		1 Truck General Stores Arrived at Railhead (Reconsigned from Barly).	D.A.D.O.S. 3rd Division 4 APR 1918
Fauquieres	5/4		1 Truck Clothing Arrived at Railhead. Moved Office & Dump to Fouquieres. 1 Wagon Amm. of S.A.A. loaned for 29th Batt. R.F.A. 61 Lewis Guns & Vy Vickers Drums from from stock for issue to Units.	D.A.D.O.S. 3rd Division 5 APR 1918
Fauquieres	6/4		1 Truck General Stores Arrived at Railhead	D.A.D.O.S. 3rd Division 6 APR 1918

3rd Div'n

WAR DIARY
or
INTELLIGENCE SUMMARY.
(Erase heading not required.)

Army Form C. 2118.

Instructions regarding War Diaries and Intelligence Summaries are contained in F. S. Regs., Part II. and the Staff Manual respectively. Title pages will be prepared in manuscript.

Place	Date	Hour	Summary of Events and Information	Remarks and references to Appendices
Houplines	7/4		1 Truck Clothing & 1 Truck General Stores arrived at Railhead. Also 1 Limbered Wagon & 1 R.T. Body for 8/1 L.B. & 1/ R.T. Body for H.Q.R.F., 1 L.B. drawn from G. Park for 8th T.M.B - 8 - 9 T.M.B -1 9. T.M.B. 14. 3" T.M. Drawn from G. Park for 8th TMB-8 - 9 TMB-1 9th TMB.	D.A.D.O.S. 3rd Division 7 APR 1918
Houplines	8/4		3 Trucks Stores arrived at Railhead. Also 1 Wagon Amm'n 1st 1st & 1 Limber Wagon G.F. 1st L.P. for H/R.F.A. & 2 Wagons Limbered G.S. for Y.M.G. Corps. Moved office & Dump to Lawrence.	D.A.D.O.S. 3rd Division 8 APR 1918
Lawrence	9/4		1 Truck Vehicles arrived at Railhead (1 Wagon Limbd G.S. for 9th L.B.) 4 Lorries taking in 2nd Blankets from 76th L.B. 2 Lorries delivering Stores to 3rd M.B.	D.A.D.O.S. 3rd Division 9 APR 1918
Lawrence	10/4		1 Truck General Stores arrived at Railhead. 1 Limber Wagon Amm'n arrived for 6th Bde R.F.A. Lorries taking in Blankets for 9th I.B. 1 Gas Mess	D.A.D.O.S. 3rd Division 10 APR 1918
Lawrence	11/4		3 Trucks General Stores arrived at Railhead. Moved office & Dump to Busnettes.	D.A.D.O.S. 3rd Division 11 APR 1918
Busnettes	12/4		No Stores arrived at Railhead. Moved Office & Dump to Burbure.	D.A.D.O.S. 3rd Division 12 APR 1918

Army Form C. 2118.

WAR DIARY
or
INTELLIGENCE SUMMARY.
(Erase heading not required.)

3rd Divl

Instructions regarding War Diaries and Intelligence Summaries are contained in F. S. Regs., Part II. and the Staff Manual respectively. Title pages will be prepared in manuscript.

Place	Date	Hour	Summary of Events and Information	Remarks and references to Appendices
Busnes	13/4		1 Truck General Stores Arrived at Railhead. 4 Vickers Guns & 8 Lewis Guns drawn from G Park for 3rd M.G. Corps & 9 YKRL	D.A.D.O.S. 3rd Division 13 APR 1918
Busnes	14/4		No Stores Arrived at Railhead. 31 Lewis Guns drawn from G.P. to complete additional scale of 4 per Batt"	D.A.D.O.S. 3rd Division 14 APR 1918
Busnes	15/4		1 Truck General Stores arrived at Railhead. 2 Lorry's removing blankets to Railhead. 1 Lorry to G.P. for L. O' Moulin.	D.A.D.O.S. 3rd Division 15 APR 1918
Busnes	16/4		1 Truck General Stores Arrived at Railhead. 4 TM "3" drawn for 8TMB. 29 Lewis Guns drawn from G.P. (M. for 9RS, 14 for 9RSF, 1 for 9KSLI) 16 APR 1918. Entered Office & dump to Labuissiere. 6 Lorries removing Blankets to Huppain	D.A.D.O.S. 3rd Division 16 APR 1918
Labuissiere	17/4		1 Truck General Stores Arrived at Railhead. 2 Lorries removing Blankets to Huppain	D.A.D.O.S. 3rd Division 17 APR 1918
Labuissiere	18/4		1 Truck Testers for Box respirators Arrived at Railhead. 1 Lorry drawing 50 Tents from G.P. ct.1.	D.A.D.O.S. 3rd Division 18 APR 1918

Army Form C. 2118.

WAR DIARY
or
INTELLIGENCE SUMMARY.
(Erase heading not required.)

Instructions regarding War Diaries and Intelligence Summaries are contained in F. S. Regs., Part II. and the Staff Manual respectively. Title pages will be prepared in manuscript.

Place	Date	Hour	Summary of Events and Information	Remarks and references to Appendices
Labeuvriere	19/4		1 Truck General Stores Arrived at Railhead	3rd Division 19 APR 1918
Labeuvriere	20/4		1 Truck General Stores Arrived at Railhead 3 Lewis Guns drawn from G.P.d C.I. (1 for 129th R.F.A 2 for 13th Wings)	D.A.D.O.S. 3rd Division 20 APR 1918
Labeuvriere	21/4		No Stores arrived at Railhead	D.A.D.O.S. 3rd Division 21 APR 1918
Labeuvriere	22/4		1 Truck Gun Stores Arrived at Railhead & 1 Truck Forage for the Wagon Lines & 1 limber Arrived for 142nd F.A & 1 Gun Dress for 130th Bde R.F.A	D.A.D.O.S. 3rd Division 22 APR 1918
Labeuvriere	23/4		1 Truck Clothing Arrived at Railhead 3 Lewis Guns received for 1st cy Ins.ts	D.A.D.O.S. 3rd Division 23 APR 1918
Labeuvriere	24/4		No Stores Arrived at Railhead	D.A.D.O.S. 3rd Division 24 APR 1918
Labeuvriere	25/4		1 limber Wagon 18 L.D. Arrived for 29th Bde R.F.A.	D.A.D.O.S. 3rd Division 25 APR 1918

Army Form C. 2118.

WAR DIARY
or
INTELLIGENCE SUMMARY.
(Erase heading not required.)

5th Sheet

Instructions regarding War Diaries and Intelligence Summaries are contained in F. S. Regs., Part II. and the Staff Manual respectively. Title pages will be prepared in manuscript.

Place	Date	Hour	Summary of Events and Information	Remarks and references to Appendices
Labeuvriere	26/4		1 Truck General Stores arrived at Railhead, also 1 R.T. body for 13th K's Liverpool Reg?.	D.A.D.O.S. 3rd Division 26 APR 1918
Labeuvriere	27/4/1918		1 Wagon Limbered G.S. for 3rd Bn. M.G.C. & 1 Cart Maltese for 4 Est. 3/S/gl. N.C. arrived at Railhead.	D.A.D.O.S. 3rd Division 27 APR 1918
Labeuvriere	28/4		1 Truck General Stores arrived at Railhead.	D.A.D.O.S. 3rd Division 28 APR 1918
Labeuvriere	29/4		1 Wagon Limbered R.E. arrived for 3/S/g. C. Co. R.E. Leather Jerkins & Undercoats for withdrawn from Infantry.	D.A.D.O.S. 3rd Division 29 APR 1918
Labeuvriere	30/4		1 Wagon Limbered G.S. 1st Limber & 7 161st Wagon arrived for 29/R.F.a. Also Similar for private units. Leather Jerkins & Undercoats for withdrawn from Remaining units & returned to Base.	D.A.D.O.S. 3rd Division 30 APR 1918

K.H.Haw. Captain
D.A.D.O.S 3rd Div

Secret

Q.M.G.
3rd Echelon

Attached please
find A.F.C. 2118 (War Diary)
for month of May 1918

A.J.Jack, Captain

D.A.D.O.S.
3rd Division
31 MAY 1918

5 Sheets

Army Form C. 2118.

D.A.D.O.S. WAR DIARY 3rd DIV.
or
INTELLIGENCE SUMMARY.
(Erase heading not required.)

Place	Date	Hour	Summary of Events and Information	Remarks and references to Appendices
Labourse	1/5		1 Truck Clothing arrived at Railhead. 6 Leaves Arms recd from G.P. for 2/R.K.R. to Camp: Scale of 12.	D.A.D.O.S. 3rd Division -1 MAY 1918
Labourse	2/5		No Stores arrived at Railhead. 1. 181 Jum recd from G.P. for 6th R.H.A. 14th Div. A.T. att'd for Rtn? 1 W.O. 1 Clerk & 1 Storeman arrived from 14/Div. Ints. 1 Lorry, to deal with Stores &c for 14/D.A.	D.A.D.O.S. 3rd Division -2 MAY 1918
Labourse	3/5		3 Trucks Gen: Stores, Horse Shoes &c arrived at Railhead	D.A.D.O.S. 3rd Division -3 MAY 1918
Labourse	4/5		2 Wagons Limbered G.S. arrived at Railhead for 4/R.F. 1 16 pr for A/4th Bgde & 1 Carr: 18 pr for 13/4th Bgde drawn from G.P. & handed over to S.O.M. 14 D.A.M.(2) for issue to units	D.A.D.O.S. 3rd Division -4 MAY 1918
Labourse	5/5		1 Truck Gen. Stores arrived at Railhead. Stores for 14/D.A. also received from 14/Div.	D.A.D.O.S. 3rd Division -5 MAY 1918

Army Form C. 2118.

WAR DIARY
or
INTELLIGENCE SUMMARY.
(Erase heading not required.)

Place	Date	Hour	Summary of Events and Information	Remarks and references to Appendices
Latourette	6/5		2 Wagons Limb: 4.5. arrived for 1 Sect. 14/DAC 1 " " 151st " 1 Limber Wagon Limb: 2 15 Pr. arrived for 1 Section	D.A.D.O.S. 3rd Division -6 MAY 1918
Latourette	7/5		No Stores arrived at Railhead 1 Lorry to Ecquedecques to collect stores from 14th Divn. for 14th D. Art.	D.A.D.O.S. 3rd Division -7 MAY 1918
Latourette	8/5		1 Truck Stores arrived at Railhead. Clothing also rec'd for 14th D.A. 50 Cutters hire drawn from 2 D Army Troops for issue to 20/K.R.R.	D.A.D.O.S. 3rd Division -8 MAY 1918
Latourette	9/5		No Stores arrived at Railhead	D.A.D.O.S 3rd Division -9 MAY 1918
Latourette	10/5		2 Trucks Horse Shoe's & General Stores arrived at Railhead 1 R.T. for 14.H. 2 Wagons GS for 2 Sect 3/DAC 2 Wagons Lim'd for 1 Sect: 3rd D.A.C.	D.A.D.O.S. 3rd Divn. 10 MAY 1918
Latourette	11/5		Ch Stores arrived at Railhead 1. 18pr piece for E/100th R.F.A., 2 Lewis Guns 1 for 2/K.R.S. & 1 for 2/M.H.L.I. drawn from G.P. 1000 Suits S.D. Clothing for Cas. Casualties drawn from XIII C Tp.	D.A.D.O.S. 3rd Division 11 MAY 1918

3rd Sheet

Army Form C. 2118.

WAR DIARY
or
INTELLIGENCE SUMMARY.
(Erase heading not required.)

Instructions regarding War Diaries and Intelligence Summaries are contained in F. S. Regs., Part II. and the Staff Manual respectively. Title pages will be prepared in manuscript.

Place	Date	Hour	Summary of Events and Information	Remarks and references to Appendices
Lebeuvrette	12/5		3 Trucks Gen. Stores arrived at Railhead. 1 Wagon Limber for arrived for Y.R.S.H. 200 pr. Gloves issued from X.H. H.C.J.S. for issue to units for use against Gelmerlinfers	D.A.D.O.S. 3rd Division 12 MAY 1918
Lebeuvrette	13/5		1 Ear-Noter for 3rd M.G.B. & 1 Cart Trollies for 1/G.W. arrived at Railhead	D.A.D.O.S. 3rd Division 13 MAY 1918
Lebeuvrette	14/5		1 Truck General Stores arrived at Railhead. Also Bicycles for A.D.M.S. 1. H.5" Gun drawn from G.P. for D.Ah.E. By A.H.A.	D.A.D.O.S. 3rd Division 14 MAY 1918
Lebeuvrette	15/5		1 Truck Clothing arrived at Railhead. 1. 18 Pr. Gun drawn from 50th D.M.T. for 6th Bde. R.F.A. 34 Lewis Guns drawn from G.P. to complete scale of 24 per Infr. Bn.	D.A.D.O.S. 3rd Division 15 MAY 1918
Lebeuvrette	16/5		1 Wagon limber R.E. Party for G.G. H.E.R.R.E. & 1/K.F. Party for 1/ H.F. arrived at Railhead. 1 Vickers Gun drawn from G.P. for 3rd Bn. M.G. Corps.	D.A.D.O.S. 3rd Division 16 MAY 1918
Lebeuvrette	17/5		3 Trucks Gen. Stores arrived at Railhead	D.A.D.O.S. 3rd Division 17 MAY 1918

4th Sheet

Army Form C. 2118.

WAR DIARY
or
INTELLIGENCE SUMMARY.
(Erase heading not required.)

Instructions regarding War Diaries and Intelligence Summaries are contained in F.S. Regs., Part II. and the Staff Manual respectively. Title pages will be prepared in manuscript.

Place	Date	Hour	Summary of Events and Information	Remarks and references to Appendices
Labeuvrière	18/5		O/No Stores arrived at Railhead	D.A.D.O.S. 3rd Division 18 MAY 1918
Labeuvrière	19/5		1 Truck General Stores arrived at Railhead 1 RT Body for 9/R.S. for 3/Sec 3/DAC received	D.A.D.O.S. 3rd Division 19 MAY 1918
Labeuvrière	20/5		O/No Stores arrived at Railhead	D.A.D.O.S. 3rd Division 20 MAY 1918
Labeuvrière	21/5		1 Truck General Stores arrived at Railhead 1 Wagon GS received for 1 Sec. 3/DAC	D.A.D.O.S. 3rd Division 21 MAY 1918
Labeuvrière	22/5		2 Trucks Clothing arrived at Railhead	D.A.D.O.S. 3rd Division 22 MAY 1918
Labeuvrière	23/5		O/No Stores arrived at Railhead 1 1st Gun drawn from 56th Workshop & launched over to 75th FHW for 147 N.A.	D.A.D.O.S. 3rd Division 23 MAY 1918
Labeuvrière	24/5		1 Truck Gen: Stores arrived at Railhead, also W.R. Trav: for H/R 4 3rd Sig. Co. R.E.	D.A.D.O.S. 3rd Division 24 MAY 1918

5th Sheet

Army Form C. 2118.

WAR DIARY
or
INTELLIGENCE SUMMARY.
(Erase heading not required.)

Instructions regarding War Diaries and Intelligence Summaries are contained in F.S. Regs., Part II. and the Staff Manual respectively. Title pages will be prepared in manuscript.

Place	Date	Hour	Summary of Events and Information	Remarks and references to Appendices.
Lakenness	25/5		No Stores Arrived at Railhead	D.A.D.O.S. 3rd Division 25 MAY 1918
Lakenness	26/5		2 Trucks General Stores Arrived at Railhead	D.A.D.O.S. 3rd Division 26 MAY 1918
Lakenness	27/5		1 Tent Bath for 3/Sig Co. 1 Water Cart for 9/H.L.I. B/2 K.R.R. 1 Wagon limb. for Same. 9/A&B.B. Arrived at Railhead. 1 15.pr Gun drawn for W.6 2MH for 6th Div A.F.A.	D.A.D.O.S. 3rd Division 27 MAY 1918
Lakenness	28/5		1 Truck Gen. Stores Arrived at Railhead	D.A.D.O.S. 3rd Division 28 MAY 1918
Lakenness	29/5		1 Truck Clothing Arrived at Railhead.	D.A.D.O.S. 3rd Division 29 MAY 1918
Lakenness	30/5		300 Lacrime Blankets Arrived for 3/San: Sect: 1 Cart load Arrived for 60 H/d C.E R.E.	D.A.D.O.S. 30 MAY 1918
Lakenness	31/5		1 Truck General Stores Arrived at Railhead	D.A.D.O.S. 3rd Division 31 MAY 1918

N. Sayer, Captain
DADOS 3rd DIV

SECRET

D.A.G.,
3rd Echelon.

> D.A.D.O.S.
> 3rd Division
> 30 JUN. 1918

   Herewith A.F., C.2118 (War Diary) for month of June, 1916, for disposal please.

                   [signature], Major.
30/6/18.   D.A.D.O.S., 3rd Division.

Army Form C. 2118.

WAR DIARY
or
INTELLIGENCE SUMMARY.

(Erase heading not required.)

Instructions regarding War Diaries and Intelligence Summaries are contained in F. S. Regs., Part II. and the Staff Manual respectively. Title pages will be prepared in manuscript.

Place	Date	Hour	Summary of Events and Information	Remarks and references to Appendices
Gavrelle	1/6/18		No Stores Arrived at Railhead. Moved Office & Dump. 230 Suits Kitskin Clothing drawn for R.A. for use against gas	D.A.D.O.S. 3rd Division 1 JUN 1918
Saqueny	2/6/18		2 Trucks General Stores received at Railhead, also 1 class Cart for M.G. Coys. & 1 Wagon G.S. for 14th D.A.C. 1 18½" gun for 1/5 Battery & 1 15 Pndr for 131st Bde. Transferred from 41	D.A.D.O.S. 3rd Division 2 JUN 1918
Saqueny	3/6/18		No Stores Arrived at Railhead	D.A.D.O.S. 3rd Division 3 JUN 1918
Saqueny	4/6/18		2 Tons Gen Stores Arrived at Railhead 1 3" TM recd from G.P. for 8/ T.M.B.	D.A.D.O.S. 3rd Division 4 JUN 1918
Saqueny	5/6/18		1 Truck Clothing Arrived at Railhead	D.A.D.O.S. 3rd Division 5 JUN 1918
Saqueny	6/6/18		30 Wheels Received from Railhead for units	D.A.D.O.S. 3rd Division 6 JUN 1918
Saqueny	7/6/18		1 Truck Eng. Stores Arrived at Railhead	D.A.D.O.S. 3rd Division 7 JUN 1918

Army Form C. 2118.

WAR DIARY
or
INTELLIGENCE SUMMARY.
(*Erase heading not required.*)

Instructions regarding War Diaries and Intelligence Summaries are contained in F. S. Regs., Part II. and the Staff Manual respectively. Title pages will be prepared in manuscript.

Place	Date	Hour	Summary of Events and Information	Remarks and references to Appendices
Sapignies	8/6		1 Wagon limbered for W.R.S.T. & 1 for H/A.T.; 1 Cart off 2/Mess for H." H/A.T. Arrived at Railhead. 12 Stores Arms drawn from G.P. to complete Sect of 32 per Inf.y Batt.n	D.A.D.O.S. 3rd Division 8 JUN 1918
Sapignies	9/6		1 Truck General Stores arrived at Railhead.	D.A.D.O.S. 3rd Division 9 JUN 1918
Sapignies	10/6		No Stores arrived at Railhead.	D.A.D.O.S. 3rd Division 10 JUN 1918
Sapignies	11/6		1 Truck Stores arrived at Railhead.	D.A.D.O.S. 3rd Division 11 JUN 1918
Sapignies	12/6		No Stores arrived at Railhead. 2) 15, 25 received for 4-5th pdr. & "B" Batt. H.L.I. 139 de. 3 Wagons Amm.n received for C" Batt: H.L.I. 139 de.	D.A.D.O.S. 3rd Division 12 JUN 1918
Sapignies	13/6		1 Truck Clothing arrived at Railhead. 2 Trucks Amm.s rec.d from Gun Park for 3rd A.G.C	D.A.D.O.S. 3rd Division 13 JUN 1918

Army Form C. 2118.

WAR DIARY
or
INTELLIGENCE SUMMARY.
(Erase heading not required.)

Place	Date	Hour	Summary of Events and Information	Remarks and references to Appendices
Lapugnoy	14/6/18		2 Truck Wheels & Horse Shoes Arrived at Railhead. 1 Wagon Ammn. 9/4/18 recd for 1 Sect. of DAC	D.A.D.O.S. 3rd Division 14 JUN 1918
Lapugnoy	15/6/18		1 Truck General Stores Arrived at Railhead. 1 Vickers Gun received for 3rd 10" M.G.C.	D.A.D.O.S. 3rd Division 15 JUN 1918
Lapugnoy	16/6/18		No Stores Arrived at Railhead.	D.A.D.O.S. 3rd Division 16 JUN 1918
Lapugnoy	17/6/18		2 Trucks - Picketing gear, Grease, oil & Paints; Box Respirators.	D.A.D.O.S. 3rd Division 17 JUN 1918
Lapugnoy	18/6/18		No Stores Arrived at Railhead. Capt. T. H. EDWARDS A.O.D. arrived for instruction in Divl Ordnance duties.	D.A.D.O.S. 3rd Division 18 JUN 1918
Lapugnoy	19/6		1 Truck Clothing, Eqpt. etc, arrived at Railhead. 1 O.O. & 2 men left for "tour of duty in England."	D.A.D.O.S. 3rd Division 19 JUN 1918
Lapugnoy	20/6		No Stores arrived.	D.A.D.O.S. 3rd Division 20 JUN 1918
Lapugnoy	21/6		1 Truck Horse Shoes, nose bags etc arrived.	3rd 21 JUN 1918

Army Form C. 2118.

WAR DIARY
or
INTELLIGENCE SUMMARY.
(Erase heading not required.)

Instructions regarding War Diaries and Intelligence Summaries are contained in F.S. Regs., Part II. and the Staff Manual respectively. Title pages will be prepared in manuscript.

Place	Date	Hour	Summary of Events and Information	Remarks and references to Appendices
Labuguy	21/6/18		No Stores arrived at Railhead.	3rd Division 22 JUN 1918 D.A.D.O.S.
Labuguy	22/6/18		1 Truck Pickering gear arrived.	3rd Division 23 JUN 1918 D.A.D.O.S.
Labuguy	24/6/18		No Stores arrived at Railhead.	3rd Division 25 JUN 1918
Labuguy	25/6/18		No Stores arrived. Capt. Edwards A.O.D. left for 37th Division.	3rd Division 26 JUN 1918 D.A.D.O.S.
Labuguy	26/6/18		3 Trucks arrived at Railhead. Clothing, General Stores, & 2 Vehicles.	3rd Division 26 JUN 1918 D.A.D.O.S.
Labuguy	27/6/18		No Stores arrived at Railhead.	3rd Division 27 JUN 1918 D.A.D.O.S.
Labuguy	28/6/18		1 Truck Horse Shoes, Nose Bags etc. arrived.	3rd Division 28 JUN 1918 D.A.D.O.S.
Labuguy	29/6/18		No Stores arrived at Railhead.	3rd Division 29 JUN 1918
Labuguy	30/6/18		1 Truck Pickering gear, viz. 5 Grease etc., 1 for 4th R. 3 & 1 for 13th K. Liverpools. 2 Limbered wagons.	D.J. Jacob. Major.

> D.A.D.O.S.
> 3rd ...
> 2 7 JUL 1916

WAR DIARY
or
INTELLIGENCE SUMMARY.

(Erase heading not required.)

Army Form C. 2118.

DADOS 3

Place	Date	Hour	Summary of Events and Information	Remarks and references to Appendices
Lapugny	July 1/18		10 Stores arrived at Railhead	3rd Division 1 JUL 1918
Lapugny	2/18		10 Stores arrived at Railhead.	D.A.D.O.S. 3rd Division 2 JUL 1918
Lapugny	3/18		6 Ton Lorks & G.S. Clothing arrived, + 1 G.S. wagon for D.A.C.	3rd Division 3 JUL 1918
Lapugny	4/18		10 Stores arrived at Railhead.	D.A.D.O.S. 3rd Division 4 JUL 1918
La Lapugny	5/18		4 Ton General Stores arrived	D.A.D.O.S. 3rd Division 5 JUL 1918
Lapugny	6/18		10 Stores arrived at Railhead.	3rd Division 6 JUL 1918
Lapugny	7/18		40 Bicycles + 4 Ton General Stores arrived at Railhead.	D.A.D.O.S. 3rd Division 7 JUL 1918
Lapugny	8/18		1 Truck with 30 Wheels also 'Limbered wagon for 2nd Suffolks arrived at Railhead.	D.A.D.O.S. 3rd Division 8 JUL 1918

Army Form C. 2118.

WAR DIARY
or
INTELLIGENCE SUMMARY.
(Erase heading not required)

Instructions regarding War Diaries and Intelligence Summaries are contained in F.S. Regs., Part II. and the Staff Manual respectively. Title pages will be prepared in manuscript.

Place	Date	Hour	Summary of Events and Information	Remarks and references to Appendices
Lapergue	August 9/18		No Stores arrived at Railhead.	3rd Division 9 JUL 1918 D.A.D.O.S
Lapergue	August 10/18	2	8 Gun General Stores arrived at Railhead.	3rd Division 10 JUL 1918 D.A.D.O.S
Lapergue	August 11/18	2	No Stores arrived at Railhead.	3rd Division 11 JUL 1918 D.A.D.O.S
Lapergue	August 12/18	2	8 Gun General Stores arrived, 7, I.E.S. wagon for 14th D Shan, wagon arrived for 3rd M.G.C.	3rd Division 12 JUL 1918 D.A.D.O.S
Lapergue	August 13/18	3	1 Hind Foolin Lurken wagon arrived for 3rd M.G.C.	3rd Division 13 JUL 1918 D.A.D.O.S
Lapergue	August 14/18	2	6 Gun General Stores arrived at Railhead also 33 Bicycle 10 Wheels.	3rd Division 14 JUL 1918 D.A.D.O.S
Lapergue	August 15/18		No Stores arrived at Railhead	3rd Division 15 JUL 1918 D.A.D.O.S
Lapergue	August 16/18	2	No Stores arrived from Pan. Gun Park lorry delivering Gun Stores 1 Italia Cart arrived for 2 Section A.T.C.	3rd Division 16 JUL 1918 D.A.D.O.S
Lapergue	August 17/18	2	10 Gun General Stores arrived, also 1 Hind Joolin Lurken wagon for 2nd R.Scots.	3rd Division 17 JUL 1918 D.A.D.O.S

Army Form C. 2118.

WAR DIARY
or
INTELLIGENCE SUMMARY.
(Erase heading not required.)

Instructions regarding War Diaries and Intelligence Summaries are contained in F. S. Regs., Part II. and the Staff Manual respectively. Title pages will be prepared in manuscript.

Place	Date	Hour	Summary of Events and Information	Remarks and references to Appendices
Lafauquet	August 18	2/15	20 wheels arrived at Railhead	D.A.D.O.S. 3rd Division 18 JUL 1918
Lafauquet	August 19	2/15	9 tons General Stores arrived at Railhead.	3rd Divn 19 JUL 1918
Lafauquet	August 20	2/15	10 Stores arrived at Railhead.	D.A.D/O.S. 3rd Divn 20 JUL 1918
Lafauquet	August 21	2/15	4 tons General Stores arrived.	D.A.D.O.S. 3rd Division 21 JUL 1918
Lafauquet	August 22	2/15	20 Stores arrived at Railhead	D.A.D.O.S. 3rd Division 22 JUL 1918
Lafauquet	August 23	2/15	10 Stores arrived at Railhead. Lorry delivering from Stores.	D.A.D.O.S. 3rd Division 23 JUL 1918
Lafauquet	August 24	2/15	8 tons General Stores arrived at Railhead.	D.A.D.O.S. 3rd Division 24 JUL 1918
Lafauquet	August 25	2/15	10 Stores arrived at Railhead. 1 G.C. Wagon for D.A.C. and 1 K.T. for Pl. Erskine arrived	D.A.D.O.S. 3rd Division 25 JUL 1918

Army Form C. 2118.

WAR DIARY
or
INTELLIGENCE SUMMARY.
(Erase heading not required.)

Instructions regarding War Diaries and Intelligence Summaries are contained in F. S. Regs., Part II. and the Staff Manual respectively. Title pages will be prepared in manuscript.

Place	Date	Hour	Summary of Events and Information	Remarks and references to Appendices
Lapugnoy	26/7		1 Com General Stores arrived at Railhead.	D.A.D.O.S. 3rd Division 26 JUL 1918
Lapugnoy	27/7		98 Stores arrived at Railhead	D.A.D.O.S. 3rd Division 27 JUL 1918
Lapugnoy	28/7		1 Com General Stores arrived – 1 G.S. Wagon for 14th D. Train	D.A.D.O.S. 3rd Division 28 JUL 1918
Lapugnoy	29/7		No Stores arrived at Railhead 2 Water Carts received (Completely dismounted) for 3rd Bn. M.G. Coy.	D.A.D.O.S. 3rd Division 29 JUL 1918
Lapugnoy	30/7		No Stores arrived at Railhead	D.A.D.O.S. 3rd Division 30 JUL 1918
Lapugnoy	31/7		No stores arrived at R.H. 1 Com General Stores arrived at Railhead	D.A.D.O.S. 3rd Division 31 JUL 1918

T. J. Green, Major.

D.A.G.,
'G.H.Q.,' 3rd Echelon.

> [stamp: D.A.D.O.S. 3rd Division 31 AUG 1918]   D.A., 53/2.

      Herewith A.F.;C.2118. for month of August, 1918 - for your retention please.

                                                     Major.

31/8/18.   D.A.D.O.S., 3rd Division.

Army Form C. 2118.

WAR DIARY
or
INTELLIGENCE SUMMARY.
(Erase heading not required.)

Instructions regarding War Diaries and Intelligence Summaries are contained in F. S. Regs., Part II. and the Staff Manual respectively. Title pages will be prepared in manuscript.

Place	Date	Hour	Summary of Events and Information	Remarks and references to Appendices
Bois de Maroeuil	1/8/18		No Stores arrived at Railhead.	D.A.D.O.S. 3rd Division 1-AUG 1918
Bois de Maroeuil	2/8/18		5 Ton General Stores arrived at Railhead.	D.A.D.O.S. 3rd Division 2-AUG 1918
Bois de Maroeuil	3/8/18		No Stores arrived at Railhead	D.A.D.O.S. 3rd Division 3-AUG 1918
Bois de Maroeuil	4/8/18		5 Tons General Stores arrived at Railhead.	D.A.D.O.S. 3rd Division 4-AUG 1918
Bois de Maroeuil	5/8/18		No Stores arrived.	D.A.D.O.S. 3rd Division 5-AUG 1918
Bois de Maroeuil, Bellery	6/8/18		No Stores arrived. Moved from Bois de Maroeuil to Bellery.	D.A.D.O.S. 3rd Division 6-AUG 1918
Bellery	7/8/18		10 Tons General Stores arrived at Railhead. Stores delivered to 8th & 9th Inf. Bdes.	D.A.D.O.S. 3rd Division 7-AUG 1918
Bellery	8/8/18		No Stores arrived at Railhead. 2 Limbered Wagons arrived for 8th K.O.L. Lancs.	D.A.D.O.S. 3rd Division 8-AUG 1918

Army Form C. 2118.

WAR DIARY
or
INTELLIGENCE SUMMARY.
(Erase heading not required.)

Instructions regarding War Diaries and Intelligence Summaries are contained in F. S. Regs., Part II. and the Staff Manual respectively. Title pages will be prepared in manuscript.

Place	Date	Hour	Summary of Events and Information	Remarks and references to Appendices
Billy.	9/8/18		7am General Stores arrived.	D.A.D.O.S. 3rd Division 9 - AUG 1918
Billy	10/8/18		8o Stores arrived at Railhead. Lorys delivering ammunition Gun Stores to H.Q & Heavy Workshops.	D.A.D.O.S. 3rd Division 10 AUG 1918
Billy	11/8/18		7am General Stores arrived at Railhead.	D.A.D.O.S 3rd Division 11 AUG 1918
Billy.	12/8/18		8o Stores arrived.	D.A.D.O.S 3rd Division 12 AUG 1918
Billy - Barincourt	13/8/18		8o Stores arrived. Moved Section Offices & Dumps from Billy to Barincourt.	D.A.D.O.S 3rd Division 13 AUG 1918
Barincourt.	14/8/18		5 am General Stores arrived.	D.A.D.O.S 3rd Division 14 AUG 1918
Barincourt	15/8/18		8o Stores arrived.	D.A.D.O.S 3rd Division 15 AUG 1918
Barincourt	16/8/18		1 Truck Predigned Stores arrived for East Riding Field Coy. R.E. Carts for 8 & 10 Fd. amb V3g6.	D.A.D.O.S. 3rd Division 16 AUG 1918

Army Form C. 2118.

WAR DIARY
or
INTELLIGENCE SUMMARY.
(Erase heading not required.)

Instructions regarding War Diaries and Intelligence Summaries are contained in F. S. Regs., Part II. and the Staff Manual respectively. Title pages will be prepared in manuscript.

Place	Date	Hour	Summary of Events and Information	Remarks and references to Appendices
Beaumont	17/8/18		So. Stores arrived.	D.A.D.O.S. 3rd Division 7 AUG. 1918
Beaumont	18/8/18		2 Lucks arrived (7 Tons General Stores + Eng. St. 1 Lucks Bridging Stores.	D.A.D.O.S. 3rd Division 18 AUG. 1918
Beaumont	19/8/18		So. Stores arrived. Lorries delivering Stores to 9th Inf. Bde.	D.A.D.O.S. 3rd Division 19 AUG. 1918
Beaumont - Saulty	20/8/18		So. Stores arrived, moved office + dump to Saulty.	D.A.D.O.S. 3rd Division 20 AUG. 1918
Saulty	21/8/18		So. Stores arrived.	D.A.D.O.S. 3rd Division 21 AUG. 1918
Saulty	22/8/18		7 Tons General Stores arrived.	D.A.D.O.S. 3rd Division 22 AUG. 1918
Saulty	23/8/18		Arrived. 1 ušali Cart for 7th *. K.S.L.I. 1 R.T. for 8th + 10. R.L. 1 wag. L. Parts for Signal Cof. 2 wagons L.S.S. for S.A.M. Sec. A.F.C.	D.A.D.O.S. 3rd Division 23 AUG. 1918
Saulty	24/8/18		So. Stores arrived at Railhead.	D.A.D.O.S. 3rd Division 24 AUG. 1918

DADOS 3
Vol 49

Army Form C. 2118.

WAR DIARY
or
INTELLIGENCE SUMMARY.
(Erase heading not required.)

Instructions regarding War Diaries and Intelligence Summaries are contained in F. S. Regs., Part II. and the Staff Manual respectively. Title pages will be prepared in manuscript.

Place	Date	Hour	Summary of Events and Information	Remarks and references to Appendices
Sault	25/8	-	5 Tons Clothing arrived	D.A.D.O.S. 3rd Division 25 AUG 1918
Sault	26/8		So Stores arrived. Lorry drawing 20 Lewis Guns from Gun Park.	D.A.D.O.S. 3rd Division 26 AUG 1918
Sault	27/8		Moved Office & dump to La Cauchie. 10 tons General Stores arrived.	D.A.D.O.S. 3rd Division 27 AUG 1918
La Cauchie	28/8		1 Water Cart & 1 Mar. Kitchen arrived for 2nd Suffolks. Refilling to Units. Advance - Boiry St Victorio Road.	D.A.D.O.S. 3rd Division 28 AUG 1918
La Cauchie / Boiry St Martin	29/8		Moved Office & Dump to Boiry St Martin.	D.A.D.O.S. 29 AUG 1918
Boiry St Martin	30/8		9 tons General Stores arrived.	D.A.D.O.S. 3rd 30 AUG 1918
Boiry St Martin	31/8		10 tons stores arrived. Various changes to Topelle.	D.A.D.O.S. 3rd Division 31 AUG 1918

W.J. Jack, Major
A.A.D.O.S. 3rd Division

WAR DIARY
or
INTELLIGENCE SUMMARY.

Army Form C. 2118.

DADOS 3D VR 50

Place	Date	Hour	Summary of Events and Information	Remarks and references to Appendices
Rouy Ch. Park	1/9/18		5 tons Clothing arrived at Railhead.	D.A.D.O.S. 3rd Division 1 SEP 1918
Rouy St. Martin	2/9/18		Sent 2 Armourers to VI Corps Salvage Dump for temporary duty.	D.A.D.O.S. 3rd Division 2 SEP 1918
Rouy St. Martin	3/9/18		No Stores arrived.	D.A.D.O.S. 3rd Division 3 SEP 1918
Rouy St. Martin	4/9/18		No Stores arrived.	D.A.D.O.S. 3rd Division 4 SEP 1918
Rouy St. Martin	5/9/18		No Stores arrived	D.A.D.O.S. 3rd Division 5 SEP 1918
Rouy St. Martin - Humbercourt	6/9/18		Moved Office & Dump to Rouy St Martin at Humbercourt	D.A.D.O.S. 3rd Division 6 SEP 1918
Humbercourt	7/9/18		No Stores arrived.	D.A.D.O.S. 3rd Division 7 SEP 1918

D.A.G., 3rd Echelon 4   D.A.D.O.S.
                                         3rd Division   D.A. 58/2.
                                         30 SEP. 1918

          Herewith A.F., C. 2118 for month of September
1918, for retention please.

                                    [signature],
                                              Major.
30.9.18.   D.A.D.O.S., 3rd Division.

Army Form C. 2118.

WAR DIARY
or
INTELLIGENCE SUMMARY.
(Erase heading not required.)

Instructions regarding War Diaries and Intelligence Summaries are contained in F. S. Regs., Part II. and the Staff Manual respectively. Title pages will be prepared in manuscript.

Place	Date	Hour	Summary of Events and Information	Remarks and references to Appendices
Humbercamp	8/9/18		17 Tons General Stores arrived. 2 Limbered wagons arrived - 1 each for 2nd Suffolks and 1st Gordons. 1 Trav. Kitchen arrived for 8th R.L. 1 water cart for 23rd Bty.	3rd Division 8 SEP 1918
Humbercamp	9/9/18		3½ Tons Clothing arrived.	D.A.D.O.S. 3rd Division 9 SEP 1918
Humbercamp	10/9/18		Tons Stores arrived.	D.A.D.O.S. 3rd Division 10 SEP 1918
Humbercamp	11/9/18		6 Tons General Stores arrived.	D.A.D.O.S. 3rd Division 11 SEP 1918
Humbercamp - Courcelles	12/9/18		Opened office & Dump at Courcelles.	3rd Division 12 SEP 1918
Courcelles	13/9/18		2½ Tons Clothing (Boots etc) arrived. Tons delivering Stores to Artillery & D.A.C.	D.A.D.O.S. 3rd Division 13 SEP 1918
Courcelles	14/9/18		Tons Stores arrived.	3rd Division 14 SEP 1918
Courcelles - Beugny	15/9/18		Tons Stores arrived. Moved office & Dump to Beugny.	3rd Division 15 SEP 1918

Army Form C. 2118.

WAR DIARY
or
INTELLIGENCE SUMMARY.
(Erase heading not required.)

Instructions regarding War Diaries and Intelligence Summaries are contained in F. S. Regs., Part II. and the Staff Manual respectively. Title pages will be prepared in manuscript.

Place	Date	Hour	Summary of Events and Information	Remarks and references to Appendices
Bengay	16/9/18		7 GS. General Store arrived also 1 wagon Limbered G.S. load for 2nd Suffolks & 1st R.S.C.	D.A.D.O.S. 3rd Division 16 SEP 1918 as
Bengay	17/9/18		No Stores arrived.	17 SEP 1918 as
Bengay	18/9/18		10 Stores arrived, 1 Cook & Hind tooling Limber 1 Limbered wagon for 3rd T.M.B. 2 Cook kitchens for 2nd R. Scots	D.A.D.O.S. 3rd Division 18 SEP 1918 as
Bengay	19/9/18		No Stores arrived.	D.A.D.O.S. 3rd Division 19 SEP 1918 as
Pouagy	20/9/18		6 Stores arrived.	20 SEP 1918 as
Pouagy	21/9/18		No Stores arrived.	21 SEP 1918 as
Pouagy	22/9/18		6 Stores arrived.	D.A.D.O.S. 3rd Division 22 SEP 1918 as

Army Form C. 2118.

WAR DIARY
or
INTELLIGENCE SUMMARY.
(Erase heading not required.)

Instructions regarding War Diaries and Intelligence Summaries are contained in F. S. Regs., Part II. and the Staff Manual respectively. Title pages will be prepared in manuscript.

Place	Date	Hour	Summary of Events and Information	Remarks and references to Appendices
Bengny	23/9/18	6	Tons General Stores arrived.	D.A.D.O.S. 3rd Division 23 SEP 1918
Bengny	24/9/18	3	Tons Clothing arrived.	D.A.D.O.S. 3rd Division 24 SEP 1918
Bengny	25/9/18		No Stores arrived.	D.A.D.O.S. 3rd Division 25 SEP 1918
Bengny	25/9/18		Q. Stores arrived.	D.A.D.O.S. 3rd Div 25 SEP 1918
Bengny	26/9/18		No Stores arrived.	D.A.D.O.S. 3rd Division 26 SEP 1918
Bengny	27/9/18		10 Tons General Stores arrived.	D.A.D.O.S. 3rd Division 27 SEP 1918
Bengny	28/9/18		Railhead changed to VELU.	D.A.D.O.S. 3rd Division 28 SEP 1918

Army Form C. 2118.

WAR DIARY
or
INTELLIGENCE SUMMARY.

(Erase heading not required.)

Instructions regarding War Diaries and Intelligence Summaries are contained in F. S. Regs., Part II. and the Staff Manual respectively. Title pages will be prepared in manuscript.

Place	Date	Hour	Summary of Events and Information	Remarks and references to Appendices
Rouy	29/9	10.	Two Clothing & Leather Schemes etc arrived.	
Rouy	30/9		Gas Capes arrived.	

J.H. Sam. Major

Army Form C. 2118.

WAR DIARY
or
INTELLIGENCE SUMMARY.
(Erase heading not required.)

Instructions regarding War Diaries and Intelligence Summaries are contained in F. S. Regs., Part II. and the Staff Manual respectively. Title pages will be prepared in manuscript.

Place	Date	Hour	Summary of Events and Information	Remarks and references to Appendices
Bapaume Cheguvin	1/10		Moved Office & troops to Cheguvin	D.A.D.O.S. 3rd Division 1 OCT 1918
Cheguvin	2/10		A.o Stores arrived.	D.A.D.O.S. 3rd Division 2 OCT 1918
Cheguvin	3/10		A.o Stores arrived. 3rd Armoured Shop detached – Armourers returned to their respective Units	D.A.D.O.S. 3rd Division 3 OCT 1918
Cheguvin	4/10		A.o Stores arrived.	D.A.D.O.S. 3rd Division 4 OCT 1918
Cheguvin	5/10		7 tons General Stores arrived.	D.A.D.O.S. 3rd Division 5 OCT 1918
Cheguvin	6/10		A.o Stores arrived.	D.A.D.O.S. 3rd Division 6 OCT 1918
Cheguvin	7/10		A.o Stores arrived	D.A.D.O.S. 3rd Division 7 OCT 1918
Cheguvin	8/10		16 tons Ammn. Cloth and 7 tons General Stores arrived	D.A.D.O.S. 3rd Division 8 OCT 1918

Army Form C. 2118.

WAR DIARY
or
INTELLIGENCE SUMMARY.
(Erase heading not required.)

Instructions regarding War Diaries and Intelligence Summaries are contained in F. S. Regs., Part II. and the Staff Manual respectively. Title pages will be prepared in manuscript.

Place	Date	Hour	Summary of Events and Information	Remarks and references to Appendices
Hermies	9/10		Arrived Office and Dump at MORCHIES	
Hermies	10/10		No Stores arrived. Issuing Stores to Artillery at MARCOING	
Hermies	11/10		No Stores arrived	
Hermies	12/10		3 Lorries Gun Oil & Grease arrived	
Hermies	13/10		6 Lorries Clothing & Boots arrived. Moved office and Dump to MARCOING	
Marcoing	14/10		No Stores arrived	
Marcoing	15/10		No Stores arrived	

Army Form C. 2118.

WAR DIARY
or
INTELLIGENCE SUMMARY.
(Erase heading not required.)

Instructions regarding War Diaries and Intelligence Summaries are contained in F.S. Regs., Part II. and the Staff Manual respectively. Title pages will be prepared in manuscript.

Place	Date	Hour	Summary of Events and Information	Remarks and references to Appendices
Marcoing	16/10	6	Lorry Spares Stores arrived	D.A.D.O.S. 3rd Division 16 OCT. 1918
Marcoing	17/10		S.A. Stores arrived. Walkout moved to Marcoing.	D.A.D.O.S. 3rd Division 17 OCT. 1918
Marcoing	18/10		2600 Blankets arrived and distributed to 76th Inf. Bde.	D.A.D.O.S. 3rd Division 18 OCT. 1918
Marcoing	19/10		S.A. Stores arrived. Refilling to Artillery Units at Beuvières.	D.A.D.O.S. 3rd Division 19 OCT. 1918
Marcoing Cattenieres	20/10		S.A. Stores arrived. Moved office and dump to CATTENIERES.	D.A.D.O.S. 3rd Division 20 OCT. 1918
Cattenieres Quiévy	21/10		Moved office & dump to QUIÉVY	D.A.D.O.S. 3rd Division 21 OCT. 1918
Quiévy	22/10		S.A. Stores arrived.	D.A.D.O.S. 3rd Division 22 OCT. 1918
Quiévy	23/10		Mattress changes CAMBRAI.	

Army Form C. 2118.

WAR DIARY
or
INTELLIGENCE SUMMARY.
(Erase heading not required.)

Instructions regarding War Diaries and Intelligence Summaries are contained in F. S. Regs., Part II. and the Staff Manual respectively. Title pages will be prepared in manuscript.

Place	Date	Hour	Summary of Events and Information	Remarks and references to Appendices
Quievy	23/10		9 Von Camel. Their arrival	D.A.D.O.S. 3rd Division 23 OCT 1918
Quievy - Glomeo	24/10		Moved office & Dump to SOLESMES.	D.A.D.O.S. 3rd Division 24 OCT 1918
SOLESMES	25/10		20 Choir arrival.	D.A.D.O.S. 3rd Division 25 OCT 1918
SOLESMES	26/10		20 Choir arrival.	D.A.D.O.S. 3rd Division 26 OCT 1918
SOLESMES	27/10		9000 Blankets arrived. 8 tons horse shoes & the like arrived.	D.A.D.O.S. 3rd Division 27 OCT 1918
SOLESMES	28/10		30 Stores arrived.	D.A.D.O.S. 3rd Division 28 OCT 1918
SOLESMES	29/10		20 Choir arrived.	D.A.D.O.S. 3rd Division 29 OCT 1918

DADOS 5

Army Form C. 2118.

WAR DIARY
or
INTELLIGENCE SUMMARY.
(Erase heading not required.)

Instructions regarding War Diaries and Intelligence Summaries are contained in F. S. Regs., Part II. and the Staff Manual respectively. Title pages will be prepared in manuscript.

Place	Date	Hour	Summary of Events and Information	Remarks and references to Appendices.
SOLESMES	30/10		6 tons Clothing and 8 tons General Stores – also 4000 Straw Bags arrived	D.A.D.O.S. 3rd Division 30 OCT 1918
SOLESMES – Quiévy	31/10		Moved Office and Dump to QUIÉVY.	D.A.D.O.S. 3rd Division 31 OCT 1918

L.J. Green, Major
D.A.D.O.S. 3rd Division

D.A.D.O.S.
3rd Division
31 OCT 1918

D.A.G.,
   3rd Echelon.

D.A. 53/2½

                Herewith A.F., C.2118 for month of
November, 1918, for retention please.

                                    Major.
30-11-18.   D.A.D.O.S., 3rd Division.

Army Form C. 2118.

WAR DIARY
or
INTELLIGENCE SUMMARY.
(Erase heading not required.)

Instructions regarding War Diaries and Intelligence Summaries are contained in F. S. Regs., Part II. and the Staff Manual respectively. Title pages will be prepared in manuscript.

Place	Date	Hour	Summary of Events and Information	Remarks and references to Appendices
QUIEVY.	1/11		No stores arrived.	
"	2/11		No stores arrived.	
"	3/11		No stores arrived.	
"	4/11		10 Tons Woollen Vests and Clothing from ROUEN arrived, also 6 Tons General Stores from HAVRE. 1 Travelling Kitchen for 3rd Battn. M.G.C. and 1 Water Cart for 142nd Field Ambce. also arrived.	
"	5/11		Lorries refilling stores to 8th and 76th Infantry Brigades at SOLESMES and ROMERIES.	
"	6/11		Refilling stores to Artillery units at LE QUESNOY.	
"	7/11		No stores arrived at Railhead.	
"	8/11		No stores arrived at Railhead.	
"	9/11		7 Tons Clothing and 12 Tons General Stores arrived. Moved Office and Dump to FRASNOY.	
FRASNOY.	10/11		No stores arrived at Railhead.	
"	11/11		No stores arrived at Railhead. Armistice signed between Allies and Germany.	
"	12/11		Refilling stores to 8th Infantry Brigade at VERTAIN and to 76th Infantry Brigade at LA LONGUEVILLE.	
"	13/11		No stores arrived at Railhead.	
"	14/11		No stores arrived at Railhead.	
"	15/11		No stores arrived at Railhead.	
"	16/11		No stores arrived at Railhead.	
"	17/11		7 Tons General stores and 5 Tons Clothing arrived.	
"	18/11		Moved Office and Dump to Sal-au-Bois.	
SOUS-LE-BOIS.	19/11		No stores arrived at Railhead.	
"	20/11		11,000 Blankets arrived at Railhead. 2,150 taken for Division, remainder sent by Lorry to GIVRY (Lorryhead).	
"	21/11		No stores arrived at Railhead. Refilling stores to 8th and 9th Infantry Brigades.	
"	22/11		Remainder of Blankets collected from GIVRY. 6 Tons general stores arrived from HAVRE.	
"	23/11		5 Tons general stores and 4 Tons Clothing arrived. Moved Office and Dump to COUSOLRE.	
COUSOLRE.	24/11		Moved Office and Dump to THUIN. Three lorries refilling stores to Artillery.	
THUIN.	25/11		Moved Office and Dump to LOUVERAL.	
LOUVERAL.	26/11		Refilling stores to 8th, 9th and 76th Infantry Brigades.	
"	27/11		Lorries collecting unserviceable Ordnance stores from Brigades.	
BIOUL.	28/11		Moved Office and Dump to BIOUL. Railhead changed to DINANT.	
"	29/11		No stores arrived; lorry posted at railhead awaiting arrival of stores.	
EMPTINNE.	30/11		Moved Office and Dump to EMPTINNE.	

A. Farr, Major,
D.A.D.O.S., 3rd Division.

D.A.G.;　　　　　　　　　　　　　　　　　　　　　　　　　D.A. 53/2.
　3rd Echelon.
_____

　　　　Herewith A.F. C.2118 for the month of December, 1918,
for retention, please.

　　　　　　　　　　　　　　　　　　　　　　　　　　　　　Major,
1/1/19.　　　　　　　　　　　　　　　　　　　D.A.D.O.S. 3rd Division.

　　　　　　　　┌─────────────┐
　　　　　　　　│ D. A. D. O. S. │
　　　　　　　　│ 3rd Division │
　　　　　　　　│ 1 - JAN. 1919 │
　　　　　　　　└─────────────┘

Army Form C. 2118.

WAR DIARY
or
INTELLIGENCE SUMMARY. for December, 1918.

(Erase heading not required.)

Instructions regarding War Diaries and Intelligence Summaries are contained in F. S. Regs., Part II. and the Staff Manual respectively. Title pages will be prepared in manuscript.

Place	Date	Hour	Summary of Events and Information	Remarks and references to Appendices
EMPTINNE.	1/12		No stores arrived at Railhead.	
"	2/12		No stores arrived at Railhead.	
"	3/12		No stores arrived at Railhead.	
"	4/12		Nine tons Clothing arrived.	
"	5/12		Moved Office and Dump to GRAND HAN.	
GRAND HAN.	6/12		Refilling stores to 8th, 9th and 76th Infantry Brigades.	
"	7/12		Refilling to Artillery. Moved Office and Dump to SALMCHATEAU. Railhead changes to BOMAL.	
SALMCHATEAU.	8/12		Railhead changes to STAVELOT. Five tons Clothing and Grindery; 8 tons general stores arrived.	
"	9/12		Refilling stores to Artillery units. 76th Infantry Brigade enters Germany.	
"	10/12		No stores arrived at Railhead.	
"	11/12		No stores arrived at Railhead.	
"	12/12		Railhead changes to WEYWERTZ.	
"	13/12		Moved Office and Dump to German Munition Factory near LOSHEIM - Germany.	
LOSHEIM.	14/12		10 tons General stores arrived at Railhead.	
"	15/12		Railhead changes to BLANKENHEIM. Refilling stores to all Brigades.	
"	16/12		Moved Office and Dump to EUSKIRCHEN. Three trucks of Boots, Clothing and general stores arrived.	
EUSKIRCHEN.	17/12		No stores arrived at Railhead. Railhead changes to EUSKIRCHEN.	
"	18/12		Railhead changes to DUREN. 4 tons general stores and 157 boxes Horseshoes arrived.	
"	19/12		Office and Dump moved to DUREN.	
DUREN.	20/12		No stores arrived at Railhead.	
"	21/12		Five tons general stores arrived at Railhead. Refilling to 76th Infantry Brigade.	
"	22/12		No General Stores at Railhead; 3 Wagons & 3 Limbers Q.F. 4.5" How. arrived for 23rd Army Bde. R.F.A., Ammunition Column.	
"	23/12		Four tons general stores arrived at Railhead.	
"	24/12		No stores arrived at Railhead.	
"	25/12		Five Tons general stores at Railhead.	
"	26/12		No Stores at Railhead.	
"	27/12		No Stores at Railhead.	
"	28/12		150 Boxes of Horse Shoes, and two tons general Stores at Railhead	
"	29/12		No Stores at Railhead.	
"	30/12		Two Tons general stores received railhead; refilling to 76th and 8th Infantry Brigades.	
"	31/12		No Stores arrived at Railhead.	

F. J. Jack. Major,
D.A.D.O.S. 3rd Division.

NORTHERN DIVISION
(LATE 3RD DIVISION)

D.A.DIR.ORD. SERVICES
1919 JAN, FEB & JUN 1919

NORTHERN DIVISION
(LATE 3RD DIVISION)

D.A.G., 6
3rd Echelon.

D.A. 53/2.

    Herewith Army Form C.2118 for the month of January 1919, for retention please.

1/2/19.

                D.A.D.O.S.
                3rd Division
                1 FEB 1919

Major,
D.A.D.O.S. 3rd Division.

D.A.D.O.S.
3rd Divl—
1 FEB 1919

Army Form C. 2118.

WAR DIARY
or
INTELLIGENCE SUMMARY.

Sheet 1.

for January 1919.

(Erase heading not required.)

Instructions regarding War Diaries and Intelligence Summaries are contained in F. S. Regs., Part II. and the Staff Manual respectively. Title pages will be prepared in manuscript.

Place	Date	Hour	Summary of Events and Information	Remarks and references to Appendices
	1919.			
DUREN.	1/1.		Thirty one vehicle wheels arrived at Railhead.	
"	2/1.		Eight tons of general stores and 104 Boxes of Horse Shoes arrived at Railhead.	
"	3/1.		No Stores at Railhead; refilling to 9th and 76th Infantry Brigades.	
"	4/1.		Six tons of general stores at railhead.	
"	5/1.		11,275 Blankets at railhead; refilling to 9th and 76th Infantry Brigades.	
"	6/1.		1,725 Blankets; 10 Tons general stores; 50 Bales Clothing, and 92 Boxes of Horse Shoes at Railhead.	
"	7/1.		No stores at railhead.	
"	8/1.		Seven tons general stores and 87 boxes of Horse Shoes at Railhead; refilling to 76th Infty. Bde.	
"	9/1.		15 Wheels at Railhead.	
"	10/1.		No Stores at Railhead; refilling to the 76th Infantry Brigade.	
"	11/1.		Ten tons general stores at railhead.	
"	12/1.		No stores at railhead.	
"	13/1.		One Wagon G.S., for Headquarters 23rd Bde. R.F.A., and eight tons general stores at Railhead. Refilling to 9th and 76th Infantry Brigades.	
"	14/1.		No Stores at railhead; refilling to 9th and 76th Infantry Brigades. Office moved from The School KURFURSTEN STRASSE to 6 BONNER PLATZ, DUREN.	
"	15/1.		Three tons general stores; 46 wheels; one Wagon G.S. for Ed.Qrs. 23rd Bde. R.F.A., at Railhead.	
"	16/1.		934 Blankets at Railhead; refilling to 76th Infty. Bde.	
"	17/1.		No stores at railhead.	
"	18/1.		Nine tons general stores at railhead.	
"	19/1.		No stores at railhead.	
"	20/1.		Three tons general stores; Two Kitchen Travelling Bodies for 4th Ryl. Fuslrs. at railhead. Refilling to 76th Infantry Brigade.	
"	21/1.		No stores at railhead; refilling to 9th Infantry Brigade.	
"	22/1.		Five tons general stores at railhead.	
"	23/1.		No stores at Railhead.	
"	24/1.		No Stores at Railhead.	
"	25/1.		Seven tons general stores at Railhead.	
"	26/1.		No stores at Railhead; refilling to 9th and 76th Infantry Brigades.	
"	27/1.		No Stores at Railhead.	
"	28/1.		No Stores at Railhead.	
"	29/1.		No Stores at Railhead.	

Army Form C. 2118.

WAR DIARY
or
INTELLIGENCE SUMMARY. for January 1919.
(Erase heading not required.)

Instructions regarding War Diaries and Intelligence Summaries are contained in F.S. Regs., Part II. and the Staff Manual respectively. Title pages will be prepared in manuscript.

Place	Date	Hour	Summary of Events and Information	Remarks and references to Appendices
	1919.			
DUREN	30/1.		Seven Tons general stores at railhead.	
"	31/1.		No Stores at railhead; refilling to 76th Infantry Brigade.	

[Signature]
Major,
D.A.D.O.S. 3rd Division.

D.A.D.O.S.
3rd Division
1 FEB. 1919

Army Form C. 2118.

D.A.D.O.S.
3rd Division
3 MAR. 1919

WAR DIARY
or
INTELLIGENCE SUMMARY. For FEBRUARY 1919.
(Erase heading not required.)

Instructions regarding War Diaries and Intelligence Summaries are contained in F. S. Regs., Part II. and the Staff Manual respectively. Title pages will be prepared in manuscript.

Vol 55

Place	Date	Hour	Summary of Events and Information	Remarks and references to Appendices
Duren.	1919. 1/2.		No stores at Railhead.	
"	2/2.		No stores at Railhead.	
"	3/2.		Clothing and Equipment drawn from Second Army Troops at Cologne. No:1	
"	4/2.		Refilling to 76th. Inf: Bde:	
"	5/2.		Refilling to 9th. Inf: Bde:	
"	6/2.		No stores at Railhead.	
"	7/2.		No stores at Railhead.	
"	8/2.		4 tons of stores at Railhead.	
"	9/2.		18 tons of stores at Railhead and 50 Soyer's Stoves. Refilling to 76th.& 8th.Bdes.	
"	10/2.		Clothing drawn from Repatriated Prisoners' of War Camp WAHN. Clothing drawn from Second A.T.No:1.	
"	11/2.		One Truck received contg: 26 Wheels and Wagon parts.	
"	12/2.		6 tons of stores at Railhead.	
"	13/2.		Refilling to 9th. and 76th. Brigades.	
"	14/2.		7 tons stores at Railhead.	
"	15/2.		No stores at Railhead.	
"	16/2.		Refilling to 9th.and 76th. Inf: Bdes:	
"	17/2.		No stores at Railhead.	
"	18/2.		10 tons of stores at Railhead.	
"	19/2.		Refilling to 9th. and 76th. Bdes:	
"	20/2.		No stores at Railhead.	
"	21/2.		Carts Water 1 for 108th. Battery R.F.A., 2 Wagons Lim: G.S. for 7th. Fd: Amb:, and 3 Wagons Lim: G.S. G.S. for 8th. Fd: Amb: at Railhead.	
"	22/2.		4 tons at Railhead.	
"	23/2.		7 tons at Railhead.	
"	24/2.		6 tons at Railhead, two 18 Pdr: Guns and Carriages for 29th. Battery R.F.A., Two Wagons ammun: Q.F.4.5" How:for 130th. Battery R.F.A., One Wagon ammun: Q.F.18 Pdr: for No: 1 Sec: 3rd. D.A.C., One Limber Q.F.18 Pdr: Wagon for 6th. Battery R.F.A. at Railhead.	
"	25/2.		Refilling to 76th. Inf: Bde: Clothing etc. drawn from Second A.T. NO: 1 at Cologne.	
"	26/2.		Refilling to 9th. Inf: Bde:	
"	27/2.		No Stores at Railhead.	
"	28/2.		2 tons of Stores and 111 Boxes H.Shoes at Railhead.	

Major,
D.A.D.O.S., 3rd. Division.

Army Form C. 2118.

WAR DIARY
or
INTELLIGENCE SUMMARY.
(Erase heading not required.)

Instructions regarding War Diaries and Intelligence Summaries are contained in F. S. Regs., Part II. and the Staff Manual respectively. Title pages will be prepared in manuscript.

Place	Date	Hour	Summary of Events and Information	Remarks and references to Appendices
Cologne. June	1.		Office Routine.	
	2.		Visited D.A.D.O.S. Northern Division and Fort IX reference Ceded and Abandoned Stores.	
	3.		Office Routine.	
	4.		Visited Corps I.C.S. No 1 & 29. Ordnance Mobile Workshops. and D.O.S.	
	5.		Visited No 1 & 29. Ordnance Mobile Workshops & Arsenal Dump of Abandoned Stores.	
	6.		Visited "Wagenhaus" dump of a.s. Coln Deutz Goods Station. H.Q. London Division & VI Corps ICS.	
	7.		Visited Arsenal, "Wagenhaus" & Coln Deutz Goods Station with A.Q.M.G.	
	8.		Office Routine.	
	9.		Visited Fort VII re abandoned Stores & Fort VI.I.C.S. with D.A. Q.M.G. & A.Q.M.G. Northern Div.	
	10.		Visited G.H.Q. D.O.S. reference promotion to W.O's and Abandoned Stores.	
	11.		Conference with D.A.D.O.S. O.O.Corps Troops, with reference to Demobilization of Personnel and Consequent promotion and transfers.	
	12.		Visited G.H.Q. D.O.S. and Laundry Officer.	
	13.		Visited G.H.Q. D.O.S. VI Corps I.C.S. and Arsenal Dump of Abandoned material.	
	14.		Office Routine.	
	15.		Office Routine.	
	16.		Visited G.H.Q. Labour Commdt. C.O.O. Cologne. & German Labour requisition Officer.	
	17.		Visited Fort VII. Corps I.C.S. & O.O. Corps Troops.	
	18.20.		Conference at D.O.S. Office.	
	21.		Office Routine.	
	22.		Visited I.C.S. & O.O. Corps Troops.	
	23.		Office Routine.	
	24.			
	25.		Visited Fort IX and D.O.S. Conference.	
	26.		Visited 111 Heavey Battery.	
	27.		Visited D.O.S.	
	28.		Visited Fort IV Corps I.C.S.	
	29.		Office Routine.	
	30.		Visited Ammunition Depot Pol I & II and Fort IX.	

L. Jaer, Major
for, Lieut-Colonel.
A.D.O.S.

www.ingramcontent.com/pod-product-compliance
Lightning Source LLC
Chambersburg PA
CBHW080921230426
43668CB00014B/2171